Beyond Capitalist Planning

Beyond Capitalist Planning

Edited by
STUART HOLLAND

41936̸28

ST. MARTIN'S PRESS
NEW YORK

© Basil Blackwell Publisher 1978

All rights reserved. For information, write:
St. Martin's Press, Inc., 175 Fifth Avenue, New York, N.Y. 10010

Printed in Great Britain

Library of Congress Catalog Card Number: 78–19586

First published in the United States of America in 1979

Library of Congress Cataloging in Publication Data

Main entry under title:

Beyond capitalist planning.

   Includes bibliographical references and index.
   1.   European Economic Community countries—Economic policy.   2.
Economic policy.   3.   Capitalism.   I.   Holland, Stuart.
HC241.2.B43   1979   338.9'0094   78–19586
ISBN 0–312–07778–5

Contents

Introduction   1

Part I *FRENCH PRINCIPLES*

  1. *The Decline of French Planning – Jacques Delors*   9
     Five Main Functions
     Three Key Periods
     The Plan and Economic Growth
     The Aim of Harmonized Development
     The New Problems of French Society
     Social Change and Socialist Planning

  2. *Towards Socialist Planning – Jacques Attali*   34
     The Ambiguities of Planning
     Planning and Crisis
     Transition to Socialist Planning
     Fundamental Change
     Planning and Implosive Development
     Planning and Complexity

Part II *ITALIAN PROSPECTS*

  3. *Capitalist Planning in Question – Franco Archibugi*   49
     Planning by Agreement
     Planning for the Eighties
     Towards Socialist Planning
     The Feasible Transition
     Transition in Perspective
     Social and Qualitative Factors

4. *Project for Socialist Planning – Giorgio Ruffolo*   69
   Economic Crisis
   Political Crisis
   Delegation, Negotiation, Arbitration
   Equality, Information, and Response
   Regulation and Organization
   Project for Socialism

Part III   GERMAN PERSPECTIVES

5. *The 'Social Market' in Crisis – Karl Georg Zinn*   85
   The Reserve Army of Labour
   Accumulation and Crisis
   Export Dependence
   Social Market Policies
   Late Keynesianism
   Big Business and the State
   The Case for Planning

6. *Perspectives for Planning – Norbert Wiezcorek*   106
   Socialization versus Social Market
   Workers' Participation Reviewed
   The Godesberg Programme
   Towards a Radical Programme
   The Mannheim Programme
   The Role of the Unions
   Planning for Change

Part IV   BRITISH MALPRACTICE

7. *Britain's Planning Problems – Thomas Balogh*   121
   The Wasted Years
   The National Economic Development Council
   The Rise and Demise of the National Plan
   Monetarism and Incomes Policy
   International Implications
   Big Business and Planning
   Public Ownership and Planning

8. *Planning Disagreements – Stuart Holland*   137
   The New Structure of Capital
   The Appeasement of Capital
   Political Resistance to Planning
   The Radical Planning Rationale
   Union Roles versus Union Rule
   Planning and Economic Power
   Political Legitimation

Part V   INTERNATIONAL POTENTIAL

9. *The International Crisis – Franco Archibugi,*
      Jacques Delors, and Stuart Holland   165
   Inflation and Crisis
   Meso-Economic Power
   Labour, Capital, and Crisis
   Private versus Social Consumption
   Crisis in Policy Formulation
   False Relationships

10. *Planning for Development – Franco Archibugi,*
      Jacques Delors, and Stuart Holland   184
   Re-defining Economic Strategy
   A New Model of Development
   Structural, Social, and Spatial Change
   Planning for Change
   Planning, Negotiation, and Agreement
   Principles and Procedures

Contributors   203

References   205

Index   215

Introduction

In the 1960s virtually every leading Western European country – with the exception of West Germany – was committed to some kind of economic planning. In practice, such planning was meant to represent a major change from the unplanned anarchic market of the interwar years of depression and slump. French planning, in particular, was taken to be a model for state intervention in a market economy, capable of adaptation and exportation abroad. For some commentators, such as Andrew Shonfield, the commitment to planning characterized not only the change from pre-war to postwar economic management, but also the difference between classic and modern capitalism.*

In the 1970s, the flight from planning has been dramatic. The main capitalist countries in Western Europe were swamped by the OPEC oil price rises, and perplexed by a combination of high unemployment, stagnant demand, falling investment, and inflation of a kind which – according to Keynesian orthodoxies – should not have occurred. Planning as the coordination of public and private interest, through a combination of indicative targets and aids and incentives, proved incapable of reversing the crisis in private confidence in key firms and industries in the economy.

The result has been a dual challenge to capitalist planning. From the Right, manichaean explanations of the crisis emerged, as from the woodwork, aiming to prove not only the futility of planning but also the wrong-mindedness of Keynesian intervention itself. Thus Milton Friedman and his allies claimed that mis-management of the money supply, high taxation, and excessive public spending were responsible for throwing the

* Andrew Shonfield, *Modern Capitalism – the Changing Balance of Public and Private Power*, OUP and the Royal Institute of International Affairs, 1965.

self-balancing mechanisms of the capitalist market into disarray. Public intervention was categorized as taboo, and private self-interest elevated to the highest totem of right-mindedness.

On the other side of the political spectrum, the European Left has argued that the efficacy of capitalist planning was in question way before the OPEC price increases and the seventies' phenomenon of 'stagflation'. Its challenge was shown in the shaping of new policies for democratic planning, in the Common Programme of the French Left in 1972, and in Labour's Programmes 1972 and 1973. As importantly, if less well known, a younger generation within the West German Social Democratic Party – the SPD – was demanding a move from capitalist market policies towards socialist planned intervention in the market. In Italy, leading planners of the sixties were themselves demanding a transformation of planning itself.

This volume includes contributions from several socialists who have been central to this new challenge from the Left, in four main Western European countries. Most of them took part in a conference on the crisis in capitalist planning at the University of Sussex in 1976, from which this book in part derives.* In key respects their contributions show a degree of convergence between theory and policy of planning on a spectrum of the Left which conventionally would be divided between 'moderates' and 'radicals'. Most of them combine a commitment to radical analysis with practical experience, at senior levels, of government and planning.

Several key themes emerge from the contributions which may disturb the orthodox. One is the argument that the mode of postwar capitalist development was itself in crisis before the oil sheiks threw a slick on our economic prospects in 1973 – a case forcefully put in relation to West Germany by Karl Georg Zinn. Another is that French planning was exported abroad from the late 1950s just when – as shown by Jacques Delors – it was facing internal crisis and decline.

* The conference was inspired by Dr. Cecil Jenkins, then Dean of the European School of the University, whose tenure of that office was a welcome illustration of the possible triumph of enlightenment over bureaucracy.

Most contributors stress the importance of the rise of big league private enterprise groups as a consequence of the period of postwar expansion, which gave its head to the monopoly trend in Western European capital, and posed new problems in the relationship between big business and the modern capitalist state. Several contributions emphasize both the extent to which such new big business power has divorced the classic macro-micro synthesis, and that only a combination of new public ownership and new forms of social control will place governments of the Left in a position to transform the criteria and use of such big business power in a socialized economy.

The question of social control is crucial. If capitalism is a mode of production based on class, then class power itself is two sided: it is a matter not only of who owns but also who controls the means of production, distribution, and exchange. The change of ownership from private capital to the state will not in itself transform the criteria or general use of resources in society. Control itself has to be transformed. The transfer of control over the use of resources from big league private capital to the state would itself tend to mean the maintenance of unchanged social and class relations, both at work and in society. Without a socialization of control, with new forms of industrial and economic democracy, and new negotiation of changed ends for the use of resources, the institutions of state ownership and planning would tend to mean corporatism or state capitalism, rather than a transition to socialist planning and socialized development.

Besides, the question of transformed control now also must mean transformed perspectives for the feasible distribution of employment and income within society. The recent scale of technical progress and the substitution of capital for labour through industry has not been matched by a range of product innovations absorbing the labour displaced by innovation in techniques. Conventional full employment has given way to major structural unemployment. The modern capitalist state since the 1960s has tried to absorb this displaced labour in public services.

But it depended on effective taxation plus continued economic growth to sustain the incomes paid in such public sector services. Also, as growth fell off, then basically failed, it decreased effective taxation by tax handouts and subsidies to the private sector, prompting a fiscal crisis of the state which further reduced its capacity to ensure sustained demand and expansion. It thus compounded the nature of its own crisis, resorting to simplist monetarist explanations to legitimize its expenditure cuts and ideological crisis.

If the European Left is to respond effectively to this crisis of ideology and state power, it must do so within perspectives for a new mode of socialized development, within a democratic framework for the planned use of resources in society. This study should show that the case for such change is not limited to one country, one party, or one fraction of the Left. It indicates a degree of convergence in theory and policy between ideologues and activists in four European parties – the French and Italian Socialists, the SPD, and the British Labour Party.

There are of course divisions and weaknesses on the European Left in these countries: between the Communists and Socialists in France and Italy, and between socialists and social democrats in Germany within the SPD and the Labour Party. In France and Italy there are major problems of legitimizing a 'socialist project' for society and gaining office. In Germany and Britain there are formidable problems of transforming the occupation of government office and the management of capitalism into the exercise of democratic power on the lines of a socialist programme.

None the less, at the level of political programmes – including the Mannheim Programme of 1975 in the SPD, as well as the Common Programme in France and Labour's Programmes 1973 and 1976 in Britain – the case for socialist planning has already been endorsed on the agenda of major parties. If government ministers hesitate in office to challenge capitalism by mobilizing such programmes for socialist planning, this partly relates to their own discredited assumptions that modern capitalism can be planned without a change in the balance of power away from capital and in favour of working people through economic democracy.

No major change in assumptions, presumptions, or sheer prejudice on socialization of the economy will come from ideas and programmes alone. None the less, ideology – in the sense of the framework of values, conceptions, presumption, and ideas on the legitimate ordering of the economy – plays a central role in the relations between the political process, the exercise of state power, and the basic relations of economic power between capital and labour itself.

If this volume helps challenge the ideology of 'managed capitalism', and illustrates the reasons for its inherent mismanagement, it may contribute to raising the confidence of activists on the European Left, in the feasibility of transforming the present political and economic crisis through a strategy for socialist planning.

It is in such a context that the final two chapters of this volume may prove of more than passing interest. In this published form, they are the responsibility of Franco Archibugi, Jacques Delors, and the editor. They represent the kind of analysis and contribution made by us to what has become known as the *Maldague Report*.*

The report, which differs in both form and some matters of substance from the chapters to this contribution, none the less advocated the case not only for short-term reflation in the EEC as a condition for viable counter-inflation policies, but also a fundamental reconsideration of the structural factors which gave rise to inflation and crisis in capitalist accumulation *before* the commodity and oil price rises of the early seventies.

The report itself, like the final chapters of this volume, differs dramatically from the analysis and policy currently pursued by the European Commission and Council of Ministers in the crisis of the seventies. It advocates reflation as a condition of disinflation, rather than deflation and public expenditure restraint as a counter-inflationary strategy. It also advocates an enlargement of the sphere of public expenditure and social consumption as a medium to long-term condition of the

* EEC Commission, Directorate General for Economic and Financial Affairs, Report of the Study Group on *Problems of Inflation*, Brussels 3 March 1976. Besides the three authors of the final chapters of this volume, the Maldague Committee included its chairman Robert Maldague, Head of the Belgian Plan; Dirk Dolman, Labour member of the Dutch parliament; and Heinz Markman, Head of the Economic Department of the West German TUC (DGB).

recovery of new forms of employment and income, within a democratized planning framework.

The report has already provoked considerable interest, not only in the continental press, but also in the Socialist Group of the European Assembly. It counters and challenges the simplist advocacy of monetary integration in the EEC as a solution to the problems of the current crisis of the Community. It also maintains that any fundamental change in the conception and implementation of economic and social policy in the EEC is only probable through *inter*national action, based on joint decision-making by national governments and parliaments, rather than through *supra*national pretensions, based on an outmoded liberal capitalist ideology.

Stuart Holland,
European School,
University of Sussex

PART I

French Principles

1

The Decline of French Planning

Jacques Delors

There are really two different factors in what is commonly referred to as 'French planning'. On the one hand, there is planning as a system of forecasting, government, and management of the economy, and on the other hand the institution of the Plan itself as a focus of animation, influence and action. Put differently, the first aspect is mainly economic and social, and the second concerns mainly the area of 'political science'. But these two features are inseparable. In France, the institution of the Plan has been created outside the framework of traditional ministries, directly attached to the executive via the Prime Minister. As a result, through such a strategic position – especially for the Commissariat du Plan – the institution of the Plan, or more briefly 'the Plan', was put in a position to play a relatively autonomous role of influence, creation and innovation.

Thus there were two essentially interrelated elements in postwar French planning. But in order to understand the meaning of the experience of planning in France over the past thirty years, one also has to take account of two essential dimensions of French society itself during this period. On the one hand, French society has always been characterized by a greater degree of state intervention than other countries.[1] Andrew Shonfield has rightly commented that this étatist tradition in French history predates the Revolution of 1789. It was stronger in some periods than others, but never far removed from the centre of government-economic relations. Because of this interventionist tradition, many researchers into French planning have wanted to make a sort of package-deal and identify the state and the Plan, as if the Plan were the expression of the economic policy of the state. Unfortunately, this was not the case. The Plan existed alongside, but parallel to, the state. There was a separate day-to-day economic policy, both conjunctural and structural, undertaken by the government, and especially by the strongpoint in the system constituted by the Ministry of Finance and Economy.

The second element that one should not lose if one wants to understand what has happened in France, and the limits of French planning, is that French society has been transformed over the past thirty years from a Malthusian, relatively underdeveloped, pre-industrial system, to an industrial one. As a result the country has experienced such sudden changes that the emerging social contradictions have been very marked. There have in practice been three reactions to this: changing the political regime, planning, and inflation. In practice, it is the last factor, inflation, which has had the last word, and has allowed a costly resolution of most of the contradictions in French society.

Five Main Functions

Besides this, there are five main goals of planning in France which have been undertaken with varying degrees of emphasis in different periods since the war. First, there was the study of a generalized market. This is to say that there has been an overall forecasting exercise, with input and output analysis of the exchange process over periods of five years, which is supposed to allow each economic agency to place itself in the overall market framework, and thus to benefit from the overall information flows of the Plan in such a way as to nourish its self-awareness, its policy, and its strategy.

Second, planning was aimed at reducing uncertainty about the future better than the market mechanism itself as a distributor of information.[3] The market often was incapable of giving such information for the medium and long term. This reduction of uncertainty, an especially important factor for those in charge of economic policy, was achieved through what could be called *publicity for a probable future*, with publication of those major decisions of public policy which would influence the period covered by the Plan, i.e. a five-year period. In other words, each economic agency or unit not only could place itself within the framework of a generalized market, but in addition would know in advance those key government policies which would themselves influence the market.

Third, it was intended that the Plan achieve a better allocation of resources – of materials, capital and labour – than could be achieved simply through the market mechanism. This feature became a main factor of discussions in the 1960s, particularly with West German economists, who debated the merits or otherwise of French planning as a means achieving an optimum allocation of resources.[4] To realize this objective, the Plan had to be able to master policy instruments of incentives and financing; it had to programme certain essential activities, and rationalize the activity of the state as central economic agent – central in the sense that it disposed, redistributed, and used public expenditure accounting for some 40 per cent of national product.

Fourth, and perhaps both more surprising and more French in character, the Plan wanted to be a privileged framework for the pursuit of social debate, for confrontation round a green beige table between forces which either would otherwise play hide-and-seek with each other, or would not meet at all in a discussion framework. For, in contrast with Britain, and contrary to some popular misconceptions, France did not have a framework of professional relations at the time which enabled representatives of the state, management, and unions to meet at an appropriate level where central economic issues might be resolved. Since such a framework did not exist outside the Plan, and since social relations were marked not only by a climate of non-communication but sometimes by virtual civil cold war, the Plan served as the framework for a tentative attempt at social dialogue on major problems.

Fifth, the Plan was thought to have the function of educating the French on the need for modernization of their society, and the imperative of industrial growth. Certainly, it played a key role in popularizing certain themes such as industrialization, regional development, and in attempts to change attitudes, beliefs, and behaviour. It is an open question as to when this role ceases to be 'education' and becomes propaganda.

Three Key Periods

Apart from these five main functions of the Plan, there were three key periods for the experience of planning in postwar France.

The first was the period of planning for economic growth. This was a period which began in 1945 and which gradually ended between 1959 and 1963. In making such distinctions I do not mean to be either very Cartesian or very French. The changing phases of French planning are similar to those Russian dolls which emerge one from another. Each phase, over several years, engendered the next. But the first was crucial. It was the period during which the Plan played a key role in helping France emerge from the pessimism of Malthusianism and in stimulating economic growth itself. From 1959 to 1963 this gave birth to a new era, which could be called that of the Plan and harmonized development. In other words, it was no longer a matter either of postwar recovery or of growth. Planning was now discussed in terms of another type of growth, and of society itself. This period, beginning in 1959–63, has not yet ended. The social factor and social questions in planning intensified in the 1970s.

This intensification in the 1970s constitutes the third main phase of postwar French planning, and could be called the period of the Plan and the new problems of French society. It is still very much an open phase. After the three crises that have shaken French society in the last ten years – the workers' and student crisis of 1968; the departure of General de Gaulle and the basically profound change in French politics in 1969; and the current economic crisis, fruit in part of the international monetary policy of the United States in 1971 and the increases in oil prices – what will happen to the institution of French planning? There are two main theses on the current crisis and

French planning, and I want to be quite clear about them, given the dialogue which now is proceeding with our communist comrades and certain socialists in France. The first thesis, supported by those I have just mentioned, is that French planning is not in fact in crisis. This argument claims that planning 'has never been so adapted to the needs of big business capital'.[5] I do not agree with such a claim. If you ask me how big business is doing today I would reply that, certainly, it is doing very nicely. But I do not think that planning in France has been conceived in the most intelligent manner to serve its interests. In developing this argument I will be seen to be partial to a second, alternative thesis on the crisis in French planning.

Planning in contemporary France is in retreat because of new conditions in French society – a new bipolarization of politics and an increase in social contradictions. For practical reasons, these factors have led those in authority to try to manage society without making call on the planning process. This does not in any sense deny the exceptionally close relations which exist between big business and the state. But the issue is different from these relations as such. Quite simply, inside the ruling class today you can find many people who will tell you that there *should be* a real form of planning, implying that the planning prevailing in practice does not correspond uniquely to the interests of big business or large scale capital.

The Plan and Economic Growth

Returning in more depth to the first period of French planning, that of the Plan and economic growth, beginning in 1945 and extending to 1959–63, one can say that throughout this period the philosophy of the First Plan, the plan of Jean Monnet, dominated thinking on economic policy. This was true through a period of great difficulties, notably the end of the period of the Fourth Republic, which was assailed at the same time by pursuit of the war in Algeria and by the persistence of major economic imbalances, with domestic inflation and a deficit on foreign trade. There were four main characteristics of French planning during this period.

In the first place, French planning allowed and stimulated the modernization of the basic economic apparatus of the country. Second, it achieved a relatively effective degree of agreement between the main partners in economic life, i.e. capital and labour. Thirdly, it certainly contributed to a better allocation of resources, which, after all, is one of the aims of economic science. Fourth and finally, the institution of planning played a positive role for the French ruling class by creating technostructures to cope with new problems.

These features can be illustrated by examples. First, in a country dominated by Malthusianism, or economic defeatism, and severely set back by the war – even if less so than some of her neighbours – it was crucial both to reconstruct and to do so by focusing on those sectors that were basic not only to economic growth, but also to the industrial tradition of prewar France. These choices were made, if not excellently, then in a generally satisfactory manner. Second, the state had or gained key instruments for a voluntarist policy. The basic sectors of electricity, coal, and gas were nationalized. Other sectors already in public ownership, such as railways, were rationalized. The social security system was enlarged, which allowed some redistribution of income. Moreover, financial resources were scarce. To allow sufficient finance, even big business needed recourse to the state, either to obtain public long-term loans or to secure fiscal concessions and incentives which allowed them to undertake investment at low cost to themselves. Otherwise, business needed state authorization to undertake a new share issue and thus raise finance on the stock market. This was a factor from which one can draw a general lesson. When finance is scarce, the planners can hold a key instrument in their hands through financial control.

In addition, planning officials, and especially the first Head of the Plan, Jean Monnet, led a victorious fight against the traditional Malthusian pessimism of French entrepreneurs. An anecdote illustrates the point. In France, as elsewhere, the managers of the big steel companies are referred to as 'the steel masters'. These steel masters were invited to get together round a lunch table by Jean Monnet in 1945. He told them that they had to reconstitute their prewar production capacity within four years. Two or more cases of heart seizure reportedly ensued among those steel masters over the age of 60, and not simply because of excess consumption at the meal. None the less, they took the point, and within a slightly longer time, by 1951, they had re-established pre-war production levels. In 1951, Jean Monnet brought them together again and said: 'All right, now another 40 per cent.' However, that did not work at all, since these steel masters had been so nourished on Malthusianism that their dominant fear was fear of over-production. In this case, the planning response was not simply financial incentives but direct intervention to change the steel cartel itself and its professional organizations in order to secure the desired results.

If you reproduce this anecdote some ten or twenty times in different industries, you begin to explain the role of the Plan during this first period. It might well be said, without implying that French businessmen are asses, that such a method amounted to plenty of carrots with a blow from the stick from time to time. Carrots via incentives to try to combat Malthusianism, to persuade people to do what they otherwise would not do, and in particular to encourage investment in new plant and equipment, while also not forgetting the stick. But these were early days in the French planning experience. Over time, the use of the stick became increasingly rare. Today, it has virtually become a museum piece.

The second main feature of early postwar planning was effective negotiation between the main partners in the system despite the lack of a structured system for such negotiation. The reason for its success lay substantially in the extent to which the planning process represented a projection of the general market. From the firm's viewpoint it meant that each decision-maker could find in the Plan those factors which would explain what was likely to happen over five years in the structure of consumption, in the infrastructure which constituted the environment of production, population trends, consumer tastes and needs. Such a study of the generalized market via the Plan was considerably superior to studies that indivdual firms might make or demand from individual government offices, because of the process of meeting, confronting different views, and continually changing the perspectives themselves.

Another main attraction of the negotiation process was the scope which it gave for announcing and confronting needs versus actual projects. The two factors combined to ensure that most senior managers, with a few exceptions, were prepared to gather around the tables of the Commissariat du Plan. One of the more marked exceptions was the automobile industry,[6] but, in general, managers came and talked. Also, the trade unions came. As a result, the Commissariat du Plan represented a kind of oasis for encounter in a desert of non-communication, and benefitted for some time from this privileged position. However, gradually, the trade unions became less interested in taking part. The most important of them, the Confederation Général du Travail (CGT), quit the committees of the Plan and did not return until the 1959–63 period. As a result, the initial enthusiasm and willingness to discuss any problem round the table gradually faltered away. It took a change of political régime, through the passage from the Fourth to the Fifth Republic, and a major effort by the French Left to popularize the issue of planning in its own way, for the unions to recover an interest in the Plan. It is worth stressing that between 1955 and 1961 the main theme of discussion on a French Left split among various parties – big and small – and between various chapels and clubs – was democratic planning conceived as a sort of political project for renewal. Among the crowd of this discussion, the trade unions showed a new interest in the Plan and during the period 1959–65 they participated more actively in its committees.[7]

The third main feature of this first period of French planning was its contribution to a better distribution of resources. Essentially, one could say that the waste of both human and financial resources during this period was restrained by planning. In the early 1960s, calculations were made to try to assess the rate of investment in France, the rate of investment in productive activity and the overall rate of growth, and the relationship between them was generally considered to be excellent. If I stress this, it is partly because today this is no longer the case. A comparison now of the rate of growth and the rate of investment shows a much less adequate relation, reflecting substantially the falling rate of profit on investment.

But in the first period of the Plan, the performance of investment and expansion was good, and indubitably improved through planning over what would have been possible through market forces alone. Certainly, there were mistakes. For example, housing was sacrificed to industrial and other investment, and simply was not a priority during the first three plans. But overall the balance was positive.

The Aim of Harmonized Development

When French planning declined towards the end of the Fourth Republic, it declined because the French were thinking of other things, because they were seized by the throat by inflation and were in major balance of payments deficit. At that stage, the Plan was not even debated by Parliament. For planners, it was the crossing of a desert. During this period, they turned their attention to improving their techniques while waiting for better days. It was shortly after, and particularly in 1959–60, that it became possible for the Plan to widen its ambitions, even if this only made more apparent the difference between published aims and actual achievements. The new directions were in three main areas. One was the improvement of techniques already mentioned. During the period we passed from discretionary planning to formalized planning. Another was the introduction of a social dimension to planning, and the third was the relation between planning and short-term economic policy which became the 'big battle' of the Plan during the years 1960–5. Put differently, during the period of transition from the first to the second phase of planning, the Plan gave the impression of a greater sophistication in its means and more publicity for its aims. It was a brilliant phase, but one full of illusions, and unhappily bound for a further decline.

The very description of this second period of French planning as the period of 'harmonized development' is intended to illustrate its increased ambition. It was marked by four main features. For one thing, France was entering into a second phase of modernization where the key factor was its opening to stimulus and competition from abroad, rather than planning itself. Second, this phase was marked by a more defined programming of the state sector. Thus, paradoxically, one saw the state focus increasingly on its own area of the economy and become decreasingly effective in planning the activities of the private sector. Third, the Plan during this period ran up against new barriers in macro-economic policy. The key imbalances in the economy continued: the Plan tried to bring its own solutions to their problems, and it failed. Fourth, planning as a process of negotiation, after a brilliant phase in 1960–5, was clearly checked in a manner that translated the committee meetings of the Plan into the equivalent of a solemn mass by those who had lost their faith.

These factors are worth elaborating. The second phase of modernization through the 'opening abroad' concerned both the decision to join the Common Market and the greater emphasis given to market forces in a general sense rather than to planning. Both factors, with the modernization itself, were to be accompanied by 'reforms'. But, again, a paradox. The reforms were proposed in documents of the Plan. Yet they entailed changes that worked towards the weakening of planning.

One of the two most important changes was in the taxation system, through the adoption of value added tax. This meant a move away from selective use of fiscal policy as a planning instrument and a move towards more neutral overall taxation policies as an incentive to the regrouping and merger of enterprise, facilities given to the finance of private investment through fiscal concessions, and advantages for saving versus consumption. The other main change was a total liberalization of the previously controlled credit system. As with the first change, this meant a reduction of the role of the Plan in influencing the investment decisions of big business, and thus its general economic policy. Also, by allowing banks to transform short-term deposits into medium- and long-term loans, it created a climate of artificial liquidity in a situation of scarce real resources, with automatic inflationary consequences. A further factor that should not be forgotten was that Georges Pompidou, both as Prime Minister and later as President, had one overriding objective: to reconcile the French with industrial life, and to promote and develop further industrialization. But this industrial policy was pursued very largely outside the framework of the Plan. It was entrusted to three or four very high level officials under the direct authority of the Prime Minister, and later the President of the Republic, after 'soundings' with the technostructure and the leaders of big business.

The three factors of the 'opening abroad', the increasing importance attributed to market forces, and the removal of key decision-making outside the planning framework, demoted planning during this second phase of modernization of the French postwar economy, which thus owed very little to the Plan itself.[8] This was despite the fact that the Plan had proposed the reforms concerned, which of course raises basic issues on who was planning what.

In fact, if there was a hard core to the Plan during this period it was certain areas in which it influenced state decision-making on the allocation of resources (rather than influencing the private sector). In 1959, the senior officials of the Plan had struggled to secure a restoration of balance between private consumption, on the one hand, and collective social needs on the other, giving rise to constant pleas for social infrastructure, social spending on education, health, cultural activities, urban planning, and rural environment. For the most part, this struggle was successful. The underlying reason was that such social spending was not simply concerned with meeting social needs, but also had a specific economic function. It created a demand favourable for productive enterprise supply *via* the programmes to improve the telephone network, the road and motorway construction programme, etc., and indirectly helped such enterprise through improvement of such services themselves.[9] As a result the Plan during this period managed to secure the acceptance of certain public expenditure pro-grammes ranging from transport and urban planning to education and health. Since it had been removed from other areas of economic management at the time, it behaved in practice like a lobby or pressure group within government in favour of social expenditure and infrastructural programmes, waging a virtually daily struggle in this respect with the final decider of such issues, the Ministry of Finance. The extent to which the Plan fulfilled its targets in particular areas of social expenditure and infrastructure varied from between 85 per cent and 95 per cent during the period. If not glorious, these are satisfactory results in view of the difficulties of realizing specific planning targets not only in France but in other countries with different planning systems.[10]

However, there was a further major area in which planning itself was definitely set back during this period: this was the barrier of macro-economic policy. The paradox emerged as follows. In 1962 the Fourth Plan came into operation, supposedly for a period of four years. It was clearly a more ambitious plan than those before it, since for the first time it integrated social objectives into its general framework. Pierre Massé, as Head of the Plan at the time, introduced it by claiming that it aimed to fulfil a less partial view of economic and social needs through the development of social infrastructure and the stress placed for the first time on transfers of social income. For these reasons, emphasis was placed on the psychological and sociological conditions for realizing the Plan. But within 18 months the then Minister of Finance, M. Giscard d'Estaing, launched his own plan – the Stabilization Plan. Nothing could more clearly illustrate the setback which planning in France had suffered than the confrontation within so short a time period of two such plans, or rather one Plan and one economic operation which was called a Plan. For they illustrated that while the Plan had increased its ambition and sought to fulfil certain aspirations of French society, it had not been able to cope directly with the solution of two pressing problems: inflation on the one hand, and foreign trade deficit on the other. And, as a result, when these joint risks to the system appeared in strength, the Plan was thrown out, like the proverbial baby with the bathwater.

In this crisis, the planners tried to climb back and take the initiative anew. They did so through three main factors which marked this period from a technical viewpoint. First, while planning so far had only projected the future on volume terms, i.e. in constant francs and without taking account of income shifts, the planners now promoted what was called 'value planning'. This meant a description of conditions for the evolution of all income and prices necessary for the realization of the economic and social objectives of the Plan. Thus, for the first time, the Fifth Plan – for 1966–70 – included a planning or programming of incomes and prices. All this struck apprehension into a government which did not want to publish targets it could not meet, into unions who found that the income projections were insufficient, and into the middle classes who, as always in France, reckoned they were getting a raw deal. But it none the less was a very important initiative.

Secondly, the planners proposed a reinforcement of the social dimension of the Plan in such a manner as to make acceptance of the prices and incomes targets more palatable. This included planning for an increase in the minimum wage and the planning of social transfers representing as much as a fifth of individual incomes. Third, since these two new elements did not seem sufficient to cope with the inflation and balance of payments problems, the planners launched themselves on an adventure which is well known in Britain: trying to make the French understand that they needed a prices and incomes policy. Despite the fact that their efforts were less rigorous than Britain's, the results were more or less the same. Thus the Commissariat du Plan took advantage of the fact that it was a sort of privileged crossroads between capital and labour to try to get an incomes policy accepted by the employers' federations, the trade unions, and the agricultural organizations. It held a major conference in 1963 and interestingly enough gained an initial minimum consensus.

Certainly, there has been much debate since on the value of the consensus. The sceptics – who have rarely been silent on the incomes policy issue – said that the unions gave their agreement because it didn't bind them and that, besides, it is one thing to say yes at the bottom of the stairs and another actually to go up. In other words, if they had really had their backs pushed to the wall, they would have refused.

But this is not my own argument. I think that the unions would have felt themselves constrained, if not to accept such a policy, at least to try it out. For one thing, they had proposed four conditions for an incomes policy. First, taxation reform. Second, a share for labour in the benefits of national economic expansion not only in the form of wage increases, but also through a say in the form of expansion of employment. In other words, if the surplus value of enterprise increased faster than wages in a given period, labour would gain a share of both the income increase and its employment potential. Third, a tripartite say with management and government in not only prices policy, but also competition policy. Fourth, a transformation of the system of collective bargaining in France. These were their four conditions.

Quite frankly, when the government grasped their implications, they were taken aback. As a result, they quickly enough consigned such terms to the cemetery of non-applied agreements. So although the unions tried to gain through the issue of a prices and incomes policy at this stage, they did not succeed. Clearly, one could have a major debate on who was to blame, but the rejection of the union proposals by the government was a very important act. One can bear in mind that as yet it had not experienced the events of May 1968, and that conservative governments normally tend to ask why they should create problems for themselves when the astrologers tell them that the forecast for the social and economic climate is calm. The negative result of rejecting the chance to negotiate with the unions on prices and incomes was crucial not only in itself but also – which has been widely neglected by many commentators – for the institution of planning. It was a key factor in the decline of planning in postwar France.

It was linked, as previously stressed, with the extent to which macro-economic policy now was pursued outside the planning framework, despite certain concessions to the planners over a brief period of a few months in which a *dirigist* policy on prices was taken as as guideline for 'value' planning. In practice, this effort was quickly abandoned. The key macro-economic policies on the budget, prices and credit no longer were integrated into the planning process. Moreover, this reflected fundamental factors which were changing at the time. With the new power relations between a stronger Ministry of Finance and the rest of the government, and changing general conceptions of society with a return to the philosophy of liberalization and market forces, it was inevitable that the Plan should become less and less credible. In effect, in increasing their ambitions for planning – to cover not only a shift to social expenditure but also the inclusion of prices and incomes – the planners virtually killed off the Plan as the central institution in economic policy.

Of course, they had some help from the government, through its refusal to take seriously the social dimensions proposed for the planning process, and refusal to negotiate an incomes policy. And in practice, French society at this time entered a phase of exacerbated social tension. After a period of relative calm in 1966–7, the explosion of May 1968 revealed the contradictions between a private liberalist mode of development and the increased social needs of the system. There was one main factor: the class struggle. But it had two main dimensions. First, there was a struggle for the redistribution of income, for better conditions of work and for the exercise of economic power. If there had been this dimension alone, the government might have coped fairly well.

But there was another dimension within the first. This was the contradiction between the new ruling class that controlled the big business in the system – what Stuart Holland has called the meso-economic sector – and the traditional middle classes of farmers, shop-keepers and small firms. The government and conservative power had need of the first to assure both their policies and their economic prosperity. But they had an absolute need of the latter in order simply to stay in power via the vote: i.e. to have more votes than the combined forces of the Left. This was their cruel dilemma, trying to reconcile the traditional middle class with the view of industrialization as perceived by the technostructure and the new ruling class. The Plan was not a good means for them to do this, since it meant transparency and coherence in objectives. But the dilemma could not be solved either through clandestine incoherence. The failure to resolve it resulted in aggravated inflation.

The New Problems of French Society

Granted such vivid contradictions, which challenged the power system itself, how could one think that planning has a future in

France? In fact, the answer to the contradictions lies precisely in planning, but with a new form, with new links between planning as a process and French society. This is related to an argument that I made earlier on the obstacles posed by the system to planning as a process of social negotiation. I have stressed the point because, especially from 1969 to 1975, such negotiation became a central issue in the new phase of planning in France. It is why I have called this the period of the Plan and the new problems of French society. To understand this phase one has to try to avoid explanations which, through simplification, become in fact dogmatic.

French society in the 1970s is characterized by economic, social and political problems which largely explain the political perspectives chosen by the President of the Republic and the decline of planning. On the economic plane, there is the cumulative impact of inflation and unemployment, whereas previously it was a problem of either unemployment or inflation rather than both at the same time. On the social plane, there was not only the background of the failure to negotiate a consensus deal in the area of prices, incomes and social distribution, but also a new phenomenon: the increasing aspiration of a large number of French people towards an alternative path of development for society. This new aspiration showed itself in different ways in the increasing dissatisfaction with the previous model of growth, in localized confrontation with the system, in major explosions of resentment. But it also showed itself by increasing problems in the working of the economic apparatus itself: an increase in absenteeism and labour turnover at work, an increase in the intensity of wage disputes, and difficulties in urban areas.

Moreover, of course, this was the phase of the new bi-polarization of French politics, with two more or less equal camps: roughly 50 per cent for the Left and 50 per cent for the Right. In such circumstances, with, for instance, only a one per cent difference between François Mitterand and Valéry Giscard-d'Estaing in the presidential election which the latter won, the government had to do everything possible in terms of avoiding the mistake, the inept announcement and the false step which could push such a marginal majority in favour of the Left. This is one of the basic reasons for the on-going decline of the Plan in France, in the sense that the government wants to keep its options open rather than to have them tied by planned commitments. Thus it always has 'projects' for this and that aspect of activity, but in practice will not plan.

In other words, there is a new refusal to plan which represents a conscious political choice. But this also tends to mean limiting pronouncements themselves, and avoiding involuntary commitment to particular courses of action of the kind which planning could represent. To put it fairly crudely, as it was put by an important politician of the 'majority' not long ago, 'the Plan is a machine for self-abuse through kicks in the backside'. In other words, the Plan is now seen by the government and the government party as a way of beating oneself with unfulfilled promises. In one sense this is a consequence of extending the real achievement of earlier plans, which fulfilled basic targets to within 85 per cent or 95 per cent, to areas where such precise percentage fulfilment was more difficult. Besides which, the French, as a nation of jurists, are prepared to consider an agreement that is only 95 per cent respected as an agreement unfulfilled, despite its favourable comparison with planning in other countries, such as those of the Eastern bloc. Also, there is a new political style in the current government which reckons that instead of announcing what one is going to do in advance, it is better to keep the project in one's pocket and, when some difficulty crops up, announce it conjuror-like with an effect of surprise and promise. Planning as a process of transparency in decision-making has thus given way to policies which seek constantly to play it off the cuff, to surprise, and to startle the political adversary.

However, the government under Giscard is not simply concerned to substitute planning by government through surprise. It also is concerned with making plain that it controls the instrument of the Plan. This is partly because very substantial criticism of the Plan has been voiced by its own majority in Parliament against the officials of Commissariat du Plan, who are variously seen by some as Boy Scout technocrats, and by others as dangerous leftists. It was to establish such control, rather than to reinforce planning, that the government established the Central Planning Council by which the President of the Republic gathered to himself all the main government ministers in a monthly meeting. To those unversed in the real power game, the establishment of this council appeared the reverse of the real situation. They could comment that 'you see how the President of the Republic concerns himself with the Plan – he talks about it each month with his ministers.' But in practice, this has meant that the work undertaken by the Commissariat du Plan has been relegated to secondary status by decisions taken in the Central Planning Council. To reinforce the point, the agenda and discussion of the presidential council rarely have anything in common with the agenda and work of the Commissariat du Plan. Indeed, the problem of controlling the planners while appearing to endorse them has been well expressed by one cynic as the wish of the President of the Republic to kill off the Plan while avoiding palpable murder.

The problem in fact has given rise to its own solution, as far as the government is concerned. For, in fact, there is no need to kill off the Plan. The same effect can be achieved by reducing it to the role of ritual incantation while depriving it of real power. This is not least because it is important for the government to be able to talk of the Plan and planning in its policies and propaganda, or because the Plan is supposed to provide a new element for realizing regional reform. Regional reform has been discussed since the early 1960s, yet has delivered few practical results. So it is crucial today to set the scenario for an arranged marriage between the interest groups in the regions and those who are concerned with the regions in the Plan. Also, by talking of the Plan without actually planning, one can attach the reputation and authority of the Plan to whatever particular initiative has been decided on by the government. For example, France today has more than a million unemployed. It is convenient to reassure the French, since indeed they need to be reassured, that the Plan has the key objective of reducing the level of unemployment.

Besides which, in the context of the government's philosophy of keeping its hands free, it nevertheless does not disdain the use of forecasting. The Commissariat du Plan continues to make forecasts, and these interest those who govern us. But in practice, navigation by visual aid has substituted for navigational science. Our leaders, and especially the President of the Republic and the Prime Minister, have always claimed to despise what they consider dogmatic or schematic approaches. And, for them, the Plan is too schematic. As a result, navigation by visual aid, i.e., by what is already in sight, has the status of a certain humility towards the future, combined with the capacity for prompt reaction to events. Clearly, to be able to react fast, one has to avoid being bound either by commitments or by any action which can compromise one's future capacity for fast reaction. Thus the policy of the 'free hand,' does not in any way mean a reduced intervention of the state in the economy. It means what I have previously called 'Giscard dirigism'. For instance, in 1975 the Citroën company, like Chrysler in Britain, was in difficulty. So the government gave it a welcome gift, a billion francs, to try to get it back on its feet and join up with Peugeot. In other words, the government intervened but, again, outside the framework of the Plan.

Put differently, if planning was in decline, this did not mean that the links between big business and the government had diminished. Another example can be given from the preceding Plan, where four industrial sectors had been given priority. During the first four years of this plan, these four sectors paid four and a half billion francs in corporation tax, but received four billion seven hundred thousand francs back in subsidies. Such figures speak for themselves in terms of the relationship between big business and the state. Moreover, if the Plan itself was in decline, it did not mean that the government, with its policy of a 'free hand', lacked individual projects. The government widened its range of sectoral plans outside the framework of the Plan itself – a 'plan' for mechanical engineering, a 'plan' for housing, and so on. In this way it maintained a certain degree of programming of public expenditure. But there were differences from planning worthy of the name. For one thing, rather than genuinely plan expenditure on education or on health, overall planning was substituted by the choice of priority programmes which alone were guaranteed budget expenditure. Secondly, such priority programmes represented only a fifth to a quarter of total state expenditure in the sectors concerned, with a fallback in committed expenditure itself.

In such ways, the government's refusal to plan was profound. For those who defended it in France, the Plan had represented a determination to master the future through a combination of political, sociological, economic and financial conditions – it was not simply a matter of economics and finance. It was a matter of shaping those social and economic conditions within which society could improve its destiny. The decline of the Plan was intimately bound with the rejection of such a philosophy. There also, of course, were those who were opposed to the concept of planning as such, but I have not opened up a critique of their position since this would demand a debate in itself. Some others argue the case that the internationalization of the French economy and the need for competitiveness on world markets made planning impossible. Others invoke the provisional character of some of the Plan's forecasts.

This is true enough; and it is no less true that enterprise needed a degree of security to which planning could contribute. One of the striking features, for example, of Stuart Holland's work on meso-economics is the argument that monopoly is in a certain sense the consequence of competition. It is partly to avoid the uncertainty of competion that big business seeks to increase its domination of the market. One can put that differently in terms of the drive for security and the need to create a controlled environment for business activities. Economic decision-making in the big league meso-economic sector, and especially investment decisions, are now too serious and too significant to be taken simply as a function of the market and without a secure overall framework. This framework, with its constraints, is the area of planning.

Another point is that the state needs a plan, both medium and long term. For example, how can one basically change health policy or education policy if there is no strategy for social change, a planning strategy, not just for five years but for ten or fifteen? It is well recognized in France that numerous reforms in these two areas have failed because of a lack of a vision for the future, and lack of a coherent strategy and periodic evaluation of the results so far achieved. Thus, both from the viewpoint of an optimum allocation of resources and from that of effectiveness in basic reforms, the State needs a plan.

Further, French society more than ever before needs a real meeting place for discussion and reflection on the future, for this society is again moving into a period of civil cold war. It is a society which functions badly, and which does not effectively debate its malaise. Certainly, there is a political theatre in which people can blame each other. But for those who want to observe and understand French society, there is less and less structured discussion that permits either analysis or new direction. This is a role which the Plan once played, and which it could play again in French society. But it is likely to do so only if the nature of both the economic and social crises, and the crisis in planning itself, are admitted at key levels in the system. In effect, it is likely only with a socialist plan.

Social Change and Socialist Planning

It is within these perspectives that the French socialists have framed an alternative strategy that aims in reality to shape a new type of society. Its policy is based on self-government. Its realization is to be through democratic planning. Such an ambitious project clearly raises fundamental questions. For instance, how can self-government or self-management be reconciled with central planning? How can the general interest of society as a whole be reconciled with particular interests, and decisions taken for themselves by groups within society?

The aims of the socialist programme may well appear utopian. But it is precisely because such a project aims for a new model of society, and because it is hard to realize, that a new strategy for social change must involve a predominant role for democratic planning, i.e. for planning as a democratic and social process for change, in which both general and particular, and central and local issues can be reconciled.

This new model of society aims to overcome the classical dichotomy between active and non-active labour, as well as the social distinction between manual and white-collar jobs, and between management and the labour force.

By viewing the matter in this way, the work situation can be put into perspective. The aim is to establish good social relations and job satisfaction. Work should not simply be to earn a living but above all to make a success of living.

This can make possible a new social organization which can in turn make it possible to overcome alienation and lead progressively towards a new human condition. The transition will be slow with many obstacles and inevitable relapses, and therefore progress should be made carefully, and in stages, through a strategy which will allow working people themselves to be the instigators of change. On this basis, a new creativity can arise, and the collective effort prove a stimulus to further creativity.

This is the main issue, which can be realized in different ways, whether it is the approach to the labour process or to the way of life which is reconsidered. In this respect, the fundamental link between the consumer system and the organization of work has to be underlined. The one is dependent on the other.

Indeed, taking collective aspirations into account – for example, the increase in freedom to organize one's own time, and the development of a community way of life – new relations can be created between people, allowing greater individual self-expression. In itself this should promote democratic activities. Hence, it should become more possible to relax tensions created by collective dissatisfaction.

Finally, in widening the aims of development, in considering new demands and social aspirations, we should be able to create new jobs and a different structure of production. This will challenge the actual financial administration and distribution of incomes, and it will offer new ways of estimating the economic and social performances of our society (for example, the study of 'social indicators').

Likewise, by creating jobs for everyone, by improving the physical environment and the content of a human work, by offering new opportunities for self-government by defining new relations between education and work, we can confront the root of the problem that arises from the capitalist organization of labour. In so doing we can transform the established hierarchy of society, and ultimately thereby promote a new dynamic society.

Self-government is characterized by two main principles: first, it should be the outcome of a change in the content and organization of labour; second, it is also the alternative to bureaucracy and concentration of power. As Montesquieu once said: 'Power will destroy power.'

At the base of the pyramid, in the enterprise, the essential self-government function should be assigned to workers and management to extend the idea of community life.[11] This arrangement will work only if the people involved can control the financial policy of their own activities and together form a coherent productive body. The self-governing sectors in this sense should be able to make independent agreements among themselves.

Much can be said about this fundamental change in the conception of enterprise; each aspect has to be considered cautiously. Certainly, many obstacles have to be overcome. Three of them are worth mentioning:

(a) the consumer situation, which is firmly established in the minds, expectations, and customs of the people.

(b) the unconscious reconstruction of inequality creeping back because of selfishness in the self-governed enterprises or because of the hierarchy which might be restored on the basis of the differences in competence and qualifications.

(c) in any enterprise, the problem of distinguishing the role of participation in the direction and management from the task of trade unions to protect the psychological and material interest of the workers.

These difficulties may well be overcome if we devote enough time to careful explanation and deliberation, if the individual task of trade unions is properly defined and if the role of enterprise is considered in a creative context between planning and the market.

In order to analyse the main point, three fundamental problems have to be mentioned:

(a) the role of the public sector and consequently, the conception of nationalization;

(b) the co-existence of planning and the market;

(c) socialist planning.

The extension of a better control of the public sector is necessary for obvious reasons: a new balance of power, the control of meso-economic enterprises, and the creation of a wide sphere for experiment in self-government. But the danger of enterprises becoming politically oriented and the rise of bureaucracy which have characterized the past experiences of too many public enterprises have to be avoided. This is the reason why the relative autonomy of those public enterprises in a planning framework has to be recognized, in order to make them able to realize social and economic objectives, under the control of planning, Parliament and therefore, of public opinion. We have to proceed warily, bearing in mind the existence in those enterprises of an independent trade union which should not be the only driving force.

With regard to the coexistence of planning and the market, the debate remains wide open. A French socialist cannot disassociate himself from the international environment and competition. Both public and private enterprises are possible means to playing a significant role in the world economy. Inside national borders, the problem might be more difficult to analyse because, as the case may be, the question is to arbitrate between the benefits on the one hand (the market is supposed to realize the best allocation of resources and to prevent bureaucracy) and the disadvantages on the other (the market has inherited the capitalist system and promotes inequality). In any case, there is a growing sphere where market forces do not exist (for example, collective services) or is not working well (for example, public purchasing, equipment, goods, raw materials).

On the whole, socialist planning means a framework for all activities. Established on a democratic basis, a socialist plan means a project for society, clearly revealing its objectives. On it there may be based many contracts between the state and enterprises, between the state and decentralized communities and between social groups, in order to guarantee a balanced development and to overcome the fundamental distortions that constantly threaten the smooth running of the economy.

It remains clear that in defining the actual process of self-government, socialism has to incorporate varying situations and possible circumstances. This would be the responsibility of the

French Left, once in government. But for the present, it is more important to underline the main challenge of socialism, and the coherence of the three basic themes of its programme: self-governed organizations, democratic planning, and a new way of life.

2

Towards Socialist Planning

Jacques Attali

There are several key issues to be considered in relating the capitalist crisis to the prospects of socialist planning in France. I shall divide my analysis into four parts. First, what is the economic and social analysis of the crisis implicit in the Common Programme of the French Left? Second, what is the place of planning now in the proposals for socialist politics and economics in France? Third, what role is played by the technical and theoretical aspects of planning during a period in which the French Left is in opposition? Fourth, what are the new dimensions for planning that can explicitly be achieved under a government of the Left?

The Ambiguities of Planning

First, why – from a socialist viewpoint – do we have to introduce the planning question into the analysis of society and economic evolution? In practice, the position of the French Left is very ambiguous with regard to planning. As has been made plain by Jacques Delors, the concept and practice of planning was an idea used by the parties of the Centre and Right for thirty years after the war. They used it in order to relate public goals and private goals. That was the use of indicative planning, to help firms with a generalized marketing system, to shape views of what the market could be in France, and to help the very centralized French administration to plan and project public expenditure. Also, the idea of planning was very closely related to a conception of the state and economic power, with the state mainly regulating and helping firms to produce.

However, such principles are completely distorted in practice. The word 'plan' is still 'on', and the organization is still supposed to be in action, but the concept is empty. Nothing is done, even in the area which is supposed to be the core of planning, that is to say, the government's own direct sphere of action. In fact, the main instrument for short-term regulation of the economy – the use of public spending – has led to the destruction of the planning system, because even its core (i.e. public spending itself) is not used in a planned way.

Thus we are confronted with a situation in which everyone, everywhere, is disappointed with the idea of planning in the very centralized and technocratic sense that it has had in France for the past thirty or so years. But we are now more than ever confronted with the need for different forms of planning, and the demand for it, when we analyse the economic crisis both in France and around the world. This different demand for a move beyond capitalist planning on the French Left now includes changed terms of reference for the debate about economic goals in our country, and the new perspectives we are trying to give to the concept of planning.

Planning and Crisis

First, the capitalist economy of France has been confronted with a long-term crisis that began in the mid 1960s, in which it has been increasingly difficult to invest and produce at a high level of concentration of capital. Leading firms need to concentrate more and to export capital. They also need to destroy more and more small companies in order to organize their new domestic level of production. The need for the greatest level of concentration leads to closer links between companies and the banking system. With a huge increase in debt, it is also increasingly difficult for firms to avoid state intervention, on all sides. Thus we see a classic problem in terms of Marxist analysis of crisis: overproduction leading to concentration.

Second, we have a crisis in the kind of production and in the type of job. In France the structure of production is not able to achieve full employment unless the level of production increases by at least five or six per cent each year. Thus, during the current recession there has been structural unemployment of around five or six per cent of the population.

The third problem is a very specific kind of inflation related to excessive inequality between social groups and classes. This is related to the capacity of the working class to defend its share of GNP, i.e. wages; the capacity of firms to defend their share, i.e. profits; and the *in*capacity of the government, of the administration, to balance wages and profits. The outcome is inflation.

Thus we have a structural crisis related to the need to increase concentration and the rate of return in terms on capital; to the structural inability of the economy to reach or to keep a full employment level; and to structural inflation used by the government and firms as a way of regulating social conflicts.

In our analysis, such a crisis could lead to three outcomes. Two are capitalist, and the third could be socialist. The first capitalist one would be that used mainly in the United States and which is beginning to spread in Europe, which is to rationalize capital or to clean out capitalism by accepting higher bankruptcies, by diminishing public expenditure, and by reducing the level of wages, hoping that this will mean a shift of resources to the so-called more productive sectors of the economy as the basis for a new period of growth.

But there is another capitalist way of getting out of the crisis, which is state intervention to cover private losses through social spending. In this way the state intervenes by helping firms to cover their debts during recession, by paying a part of their wages bill, covering a share of their social security contributions, and in general contributing to their operating costs. Such a nominal socialization of costs is not in any real sense socialist, because it helps firms in the private sector to make profits on goods or services which they have decided to undertake, on their own private and capitalist criteria. Related to this is the intervention of the state to try to change the relationship between the work force and job needs through public enterprise intervention. Again, public enterprise might itself appear socialist in character, but is not. For the French Left today, a formula of nationalization and state intervention not only is not socialist but could be a trap for socialists. Public ownership and state intervention may be necessary means for socialist ends, but are not socialist in themselves.

Transition to Socialist Planning

This brings me to the third possible solution to the crisis: the socialist solution. This raises two key issues – how to strengthen the economy without imposing the costs for that strength on the working class, and how to organize a change in the relations of power and the nature of production in society. We think that these are two of the main problems of transition to a socialist society, just as we think that planning is the only way to organize it. But we have to give a completely different meaning to the word 'planning' from that which it already has in either capitalist countries such as France, or the so-called socialist countries of Eastern Europe. These issues relate to the wider framework of problems entailed in advocating the case for socialist planning during a period of political opposition by the Socialist Party.

There is no doubt that the issues concerned are difficult to communicate. For instance, it is important to make plain that in order to increase the efficiency or effectiveness of an economy, it is not necessary to increase the exploitation of labour, or its productivity. What is needed is to organize the economy differently. A more efficient or effective use of economic resources, under socialist planning, could be achieved in at least two ways. One is to save capital or investment, and use it more efficiently. This should involve, *inter alia*, the more efficient social use of innovation and technical progress – not restricting it to one or another private company, but diffusing it through the economy and society as a whole.

But there also is another way: to ask, What is the meaning of increased economic efficiency? Is it the efficiency of more production of added value or the different efficiency of producing welfare? And if we understanding it in terms of producing welfare we can understand that productivity itself – as a concept – is highly ideological in the sense that, under

capitalism, it relates only to more efficient ways of producing or
serving existing patterns of demand. For instance, when you say
that something is productive, you say it in terms of a particular
demand that people are in a position to command. But this
demand is related to the kinds of wages or income that people
have, and a given structure of production. If you want to change
the meaning of welfare, you have first to change the distribution
of income, and with another kind of distribution of income
there is a different kind of demand. This entails another kind of
production demanded, which in turn opens up another
conception of productivity.

On the French Left, it is considered impossible to imagine
change in the structure of production and an approach to full
employment without change in the structure of demand and
production. It is an illusion to think you can do anything on the
industrial side if you don't simultaneously change the kind of
goods and the kind of services people ask for. In other words, we
really think societies could achieve new services and collective
goods if the social organization and distribution of income and
power were different. But you cannot change the demand and
supply separately. You have to do it simultaneously. And this
means real planning. You have to change the organization of
industry and services, with a change in the nature of demand
both in the ideological and in the economic senses, which means
a redistribution of income, and a new 'legitimacy'.

But in terms of the French Left, one has to distinguish
between two parties, since we have increasingly a bi-party
situation between the Communists and the Socialists. For one
party – the Communists – the nationalization of the economy
and the socialization of the means of production in itself means
socialism. It is not only a main condition but *the* condition for a
socialist mode of production. The socialists add two others. One
is planning itself and the other is self-management or *auto-
gestion*. Such self-management is not only a matter of what
happens within an enterprise, but also the way in which the
planning process itself is managed.

For instance, I have argued that to transcend this economic
crisis without increasing exploitation of the working class, we
have to change both the nature of production on the supply side

and the nature of consumption and demand. But this raises a
key ideological question of legitimacy: both the legitimacy of
the new demand and of new forms of managing production.
From a historical point of view the market mechanism has
established a kind of legitimacy which is the equivalent of the
legitimacy of representative government. Another kind of
legitimacy is that claimed by central planning of resources,
which means having a referee, or a god, who knows everything
and will decide what should be had by whom.

As French socialists, we deny that either the market
mechanism or a central plan can any longer legitimately decide
or organize that change in production and consumption which
is necessary to transcend the current crisis. We believe that the
only solution is to go for a new kind of planning with a new
legitimacy, changing the nature of production and the relation
between man and his work, decentralizing decisions in the
planning system as much as possible at every level, and
achieving a form of self-reliant production and demand, both in
firms and industries, and at the level of regions and localities. In
essence, this is the main difference between the two concepts of
legitimacy of production and demand between the two main
parties of the Left in France.

In terms of instruments or means for planning, it is clear
to us that nothing could be done in terms of reorienting
production without control by the state of at least 50 per cent of
investment. That is the reason why in our Common Programme
in France, we propose to nationalize nine of the main private
enterprise groups, which, in addition to the existing public
sector, would result in public control of some 50 per cent of
investment. Already in France the main energy sector, banking
sector, and transport sector are nationalized, but the key
industrial companies and principal investment banks are not,
and that is the main goal of future nationalization.

Fundamental Change

But we do not think that in itself is enough, nor that it would in
itself solve our problems. According to us, what now has to be

done amounts to a calendar of change involving a new relationship between the trade unions, the parties of the Left, and the economic system. No change should be initiated in the economy without close negotiation with the unions. In itself, this would contrast with the relative exclusion of unions from the planning process in France for key periods since the war. Besides this, we simultaneously have to change two things: the distribution of wealth and the distribution of power.

These fundamental changes will take time. Also, the longer the Right stays in power during this crisis of the system, the longer it would take for a future Left government to implement these changes. When the Leftist parties are in opposition they have to explain both the potential of real planning and their belief that nothing can be done without structural transformation, change of ownership, and a new relationship between growth, production, employment, and the nature of goods and services in the economy. This means extending the new legitimacy, in two senses: a legitimacy within the firm related to workers' control, and a legitimacy for public spending and planning itself.

It is important to stress that the new conception of planning is both strong and decentralized. You can do nothing without real planning powers, including the power to say to particular firms that particular activities are going to be developed while others are going to be phased out. This means major sectoral and structural change. This is a difficult thing to do, but when you have decided to help this particular sector you may have to say that you cannot support this other. And such selective choice concerns all major aspects of social and economic life. Of course selection in this sense is undertaken now, under capitalism, through the working of the market. In a social sense such selection is blind or unconscious, since society does not choose in a conscious sense, or consult the interested groups and classes in society. Making the choice conscious and explicit, within a framework of enlarged debate on the use of resources in society, is one of the major merits of socialist planning.

Such planning mechanisms would not mean avoidance of error. But if mistakes are made and wrong decisions taken, they will at least be taken democratically, with a widened chance for the avoidance of error. This potential and this horizon for genuine democratic debate – through planning – have to be related to the role of representative democratic institutions in the system. For instance, one of the reasons why planning is so little trusted in our countries is that no government at present wants to take the risk of open decision-making. If socialist planning is to achieve a new legitimacy it must overcome this through promoting the scope for change within the system itself, by people themselves. And this relates to the question of decentralized formulation of planning.

A key factor is that democratic planning has to be decentralized in its preparation, but strong in its execution. For instance, the kind of changes which would be needed within ten to fifteen years of the advent of a socialist government in France would be enormous. They cover the kind of goods produced, the organization and relations between the public and private sectors, the distribution of wealth and income, the structure of production and services, and so forth. Such major change has to involve the widest possible range of views in its formulation if the results – once decided – are to command consent. But, once decided democratically, the implementation of the choices has to be strong; it also needs to be coordinated centrally over time. As part of the democratic process it both is important to explain and advocate this, and to make clear that the absence of planning in a period of economic crisis, such as we are experiencing now, does not mean the absence of state intervention. The choice is not simply between the market and planning, but between different kinds of planning. Without the process of a democratic socialist plan, the state will intervene with another kind of planning – fascist in character – which is the last resort and last solution for defence of the capitalism system. Such fascist intervention would use the tools of planning without its democratic legitimacy.

Planning and Implosive Development

If we think ahead, to the shape of planning during the period of transition, we can establish new principles relating decentralization in the preparation of a plan to centralization in its execution. This concerns both new 'signals' which the state must emit in the formulation of the plan and new institutional networks which it must control. But the transition to decentralization and self-management demands much more. In particular, the character of the new institutional networks, and their dynamic principles, have to be considered in relation to a new model of society. This would be a framework of *im*plosive development rather than the *ex*plosive growth of capitalism.[1]

The explosive growth of capitalism is characterized by the expansion of the market and, in Marxist terms, the exchange value of goods. An implosive model of development, by contrast, would be concerned with the maximization of use values rather than profits. Explosive exchange values and implosive use values can be compatible at relatively low levels of development. But with growth, the explosive process of resource allocation leads to saturation, congestion, and degradation of use values. This is illustrated by, for example, planned obsolescence and the creation of induced want through advertising, urban congestion and a degraded environment for living. But it is also illustrated through the waste of resources, especially energy, on a major scale.[2] Inflation is the false response of the capitalist system to such explosive growth. Money is the principal 'signal' in a capitalist society, and becomes the symptom of basic disorder in the system itself. Each scarcity, each in the absence of a social process of negotiation, conflicts with each degradation of the environment; each issue of distribution between social groups, regions, or generations is reflected today in the monetary field.

An implosive process of development would amount essentially to 'anti-explosion' in the above senses. In practice, just as explosive growth is capitalist in character, implosive development in the real sense could only be socialist. Over the long term, implosive development could entail either low growth or negative growth by the standards of the main indicator of capitalist explosive growth: GNP. In the short term, in a transitional period, it would demand considerable intitial growth. The comparison between the two models is not that between capitalist growth and the economic system of state socialist countries to date, which has been based essentially on production, with centralized state control. Put simply, an implosive model of development is incompatible with the centralized management of resources as such, rather than a combination of decentralized formulation with centralized implementation.[3]

One of the key principles in an implosive model of development would be self-management and reorganization through *anti*-organization. The paradox can be explained both by the distinction between the preparation of a plan under socialism and by the subsequent stage of its implementation. But it also can be illustrated by other factors. For instance, in either a public or private company in capitalist society, technical, economic, and social information is reserved to the controllers of capital. This actually blocks and atrophies the process of communication and the effective use of skills and potential. By contrast, with an implosive model of development, both workers and citizens should have access to information of a kind at present reserved for the controllers of capital alone. In this way, new rights to both information and communication would be established. The processes, instead of being one-way, as at present, would become two-way, opening the feasibility of a process of social negotiation of the use of resources in society. In such a manner, the principal 'signals' of the economy would be registered through democratic processes, rather than through the capitalist medium of money and the market. An extended social and economic dialogue would substitute the present dialogue of the deaf.

These new relationships within the economy and society would be focused in the practice of self-management. In principle, self-management would legitimize the exercise of power in a planned, socialist society. But self-management would not be restricted simply to the sphere of production. It also would extend to the other areas of society, including democratization of the political process at national and local levels and in the social services, such as education. There are already practical examples of the feasibility of self-management at the level of production and urban planning. The extension to national issues such as taxation and the distribution of aggregate resources have become more feasible with the sophistication of modern techniques of data collection and processing. Transition to planning, as such a process of social negotiation of new alternatives for society, clearly could not be an overnight business. But the new two-way relationships made possible by an implosive model of development would create a raised consciousness of the potential gains from the system.

There clearly would be the question of the exercise of responsibility within self-managed enterprise. It is crucial that the collective owners of a self-managed autonomous enterprise should have access to all relevant economic and social information, and should exercise control through elected representatives over matters such as calculation of the rate of return, the definitions of conditions and duration of work, the rate of investment and the internal distribution of income. Representatives should be accountable *a posteriori* for their strategic decisions to the work force of the enterprise, at regular intervals.

Planning and Complexity

In democratized, two-way relationships in society, increased complexity in decision-making not only would be inevitable but desirable. It would represent the opening of a large number of new channels of communication, increasing interdependence between sub-systems in the system as a whole. This is the only way to evaluate those decisions which, under explosive growth, lead to wastage of resources and degradation of the social and economic environment.

The socialist plan should be the global framework and vision for this increased complexity of decision-making. It would not be justified by the criteria of capitalist planning, with its explosive model of growth, but by its liberalization of use values within society, and through the extension of democracy. Its role can be that of 'self-reorganization' in the sense that it can and should give the system control over itself and allow it to react to external information. Through planning, people would become masters of the instruments of information.

For the state, as for the enterprise, a complex plan should ideally assure at least four functions. In addition to self-management, they are:

Self-sufficiency. Unplanned consumption and production entail the expenditure of energy to assure interdependence. For instance, the lack of an urban plan increases transport costs; the lack of an education plan wastes teaching power. Global planning on an implosive basis is necessary to counter inflation and the costs of explosive growth.

Autonomy. The establishment of effective autonomy, as a condition for self-sufficiency, demands a consistent choice of sectors to be given priority development in the framework of a distinction between the national and international world economies. This means a strategy for selectivity in state economic policy. It also means control of a sufficient number of large financial and technological companies – the big league firms – to ensure that the national economy can produce a sufficiently diversified range of goods to cope effectively with import competition.

Self-transformation. This relates to the wider question of creating increased diversity in society, and transforming the role of the individual in organizations. It is a question of the quality of life both at work and outside it, including the status of women in society and the status of immigrant workers and other minorities. It also concerns the transformation of the present various inequalities in society into new diverse relationships at the political, economic and social level levels.

These characteristics are essential. But they cannot assume a completely heterogeneous form, since they must be related to prove effective. The new 'relational' planning will need technical sophistication of a high level in its information flows. Nevertheless, its structures and instruments of decision making must remain basically simple, intelligible, and political. It is only in such a way that they can be non-mystifying and creative.

Information is crucial in the sense that no organization can survive unless it is capable of responding to the 'sounds' given out by its environment, and is capable of modifying its structure. The information networks concerned cannot be only 'official' ones; otherwise the only decisions taken will be those that pass through such official channels, i.e., decisions extrapolating the past and reinforcing central power. If, by contrast, the state can listen to the 'sounds' of society itself, if it can promote creativity, and if self-managed authorities can translate these into action, the future possibilities for society are more numerous, if as yet unknown, than those which are transmitted by the dominant system today.[4]

PART II

Italian Prospects

3

Capitalist Planning in Question

Franco Archibugi

I want to focus my contribution to the issue of capitalist planning – and beyond – in the following main ways: first, a relatively brief and personal evaluation of the problems of planning in Italy, especially since the mid-1960s; second, a consideration of what really can be meant by socialist as distinct from capitalist planning; third, the feasibility of transforming capitalist planning; fourth, the transitional planning problem in historical perspective; fifth, the kind of social indicators that would have to be taken into account in a new mode of socialist planning.

I shall being with the experience of planning in Italy. Like other Western European countries, Italy had a reconstruction programme, which some have chosen to grace with the title of a 'plan'.[1] But in practice, this was more a shopping list of items for the basket of goods needed for postwar recovery. It did not establish planning at the heart of the process of resource allocation, even under the exceptional postwar political situation. Then, again, in the mid-1950s, the name and title of 'plan' was commonly associated with the ten-year project for the Italian economy introduced by the Christian Democrats, and popularly known as the 'Vanoni Plan'. But in both fact and real title, the so-called Vanoni Plan was a 'framework for reasoning' about the longer term prospects of an economy experiencing what Jacques Attali would call 'explosive' growth.[2] The explosion, in terms of increasing regional imbalance between North and South, balance of payments difficulties, and wage pressure on profits, was resounding by the early 1960s. It echoed clearly in a series of debates on planning in the Italian parliament in that period, which showed that reasoning alone was no political substitute for active planning.[3]

The attempt at planning in a meaningful sense got off the ground in the mid-1960s, with the opening to the Centre-Left, and the pressure from the Socialist Party for planning mechanisms worthy of the name. However, this was precisely the period at which the first evidence became available on a global European scale that the postwar expansion was in crisis, and faltering. Put simply, if the crisis and its impact on Italy in part were responsible for challenging the hegemony of the Christian Democratic Party, and opening the way for the Centre-Left, it either was not the 'right moment' for planning of the kind conceived at the time, or was the wrong kind of plan, or a good deal of both. In effect, the timing and nature of events were classic, perfectly reflecting Thomas Balogh's aphorism that when you *could* plan you don't and when you *do* plan, you can't – at least under a capitalist system.[4]

This first five-year plan in Italy was supposed to cover the period 1965–9. After a delay in adoption, its period in fact was extended to 1966–70.[5] This planning exercise, known as the Pieraccini Plan, was constructed with an aggregate or macro-economic framework, and with the traditional variables of national economic accounting. In these respects it was very similar to the planning exercise of the British National Economic Development Council which had shortly preceded it. It also embodied a list of qualitative statements about the possibilities for change in the economy and administration.

Planning by Agreement

Frankly, the Pieraccini Plan was very inadequate. For one thing it was too short-term. For another, it failed to develop adequate means for bridging the gap between the macro and micro sectors, or at least between macro-economic targets and the operational bodies or institutions necessary to ensure a genuinely planned coordination of resources.

Nevertheless, it did develop one such framework or approach that showed considerable initial promise. This was the process of *contrattazione programmatica*, focused on what Stuart Holland has called the meso- economic sector, and especially big-league public enterprise. It was similar to, and it partly inspired, what later emerged in British Labour Party policy as Planning Agreements, with the crucial difference that it was not originally envisaged that trade unions should play a key role in their negotiation.

An official paper of the Ministry of the Budget and Economic Planning in 1968 (*Relazione previsionale e programmatica*) admitted that the system of incentives in operation in regional policy had not been able to promote sufficient manufacturing investment in the South, nor to ensure the location of a set of interrelated initiatives in a specific area. It argued that a new kind of agreement between government and big business was necessary to achieve this result. These agreements were basically founded on an exchange of information between government (about the infrastructure it could provide) and enterprise (on the new initiatives which a firm or group of firms could establish in a particular area). In principle, by means of this exchange of information, it would be possible to provide and realize a better match between the government contribution, on the one hand, and interrelated investment projects, on the other. It was intended that medium- and small-scale enterprise would be wedded with the Planning Agreements with big business. The agreements therefore were intended to solve the problem of coordinating corporate planning needs with the overall planning objectives of the government.

The government intended to use more flexible incentives to persuade enterprises to coordinate their programmes and realize interrelated investment in the industrial zones. The enterprises that accepted this procedure and agreed on this kind of coordination would be priviledged in the allocation and size of incentives.

But, although the instrument of *contrattazione programmatica* had its own logic, in practice it proved unable to organize relations with small and medium enterprises.[6] And because of the absence on the government side of a clear, precise and consistent framework of references about targets, the government itself was not in a position to resist the entrepreneurial initiatives of big business, to control and stipulate its sectoral and locational direction, or to avoid its degeneration into the 'patronage' system.

At any rate, in the period 1969–71 there was a large increase of investment in the Mezzogiorno, both in absolute terms and in comparison with national investment. This was a considerable achievement, granted both the recession in private investment in general during the period and the fact that industrial investment in the Mezzogiorno had fallen in both absolute and relative terms in the previous period 1965–8.

Overall, the experience of *contrattazione programmatica* can be divided into four periods.

The first (1968–9) was the 'start-up' period in which important investment was undertaken in basic and derived chemicals and mechanical engineering. The latter included the Alfa-Sud motor vehicle complex at Pozzuoli near Naples, and a new initiative by Fiat.

The second (1970–1) was a period of 'investment packages' formulated regionally in response to particular social problems and pressures, as at Battipaglia and Reggio Calabria. In both these cases, basic and derived chemicals and steel predominated, absorbing 96 per cent of the investment undertaken.

The third was a 'break' phase, in which only very modest decisions were taken, almost all in basic chemicals.

The fourth (since 1974) has been a period in which a major volume of agreements has been concluded, but again almost exclusively in the chemical and steel sectors.

There are two major comments to be made on this experience. For one thing, nearly all the investment actually negotiated through a Planning Agreements type formula during this period was in public sector activity. The IRI State Holding Company was responsible for both the Alfra-Sud initiative and investment in steel, while the ENI State Holding dominated the investment in chemicals. There is little doubt that the framework was effective in this sense for the public sector, but the government failed to use it for the necessary parallel mobilization of big league private sector investment.

Further, because of the sectoral concentration of public sector activity in basic heavy industries such as steel and chemicals, most of the activity located in the Mezzogiorno during this period was highly capital intensive. This point can be exaggerated. The Alfa-Sud project was notable investment in a high job creating programme. Also, it has been estimated that some 100,000 new jobs were created overall. Nevertheless, the average capital cost per job was high for the investment programmes considered overall: some 80 million lire per worker. In addition, with the trend through technical progress to increasing capital intensity, the revision of projects over time, through a procedure known as 'conformity advice,' tended to increase capital-labour ratios.

In addition, the institutional procedures for *contrattazione programmatica* were perverted over time. It had been intended that all decisions taken through the new institution should be coordinated by the Inter-Ministerial Committee for Economic Planning (CIPE). This was part of the initial intention to relate job creation in the Mezzogiorno to national investment planning and resource use. But in practice, decisions on modification of initial projects through the 'conformity advice' procedure were taken independently by the Minister for the Mezzogiorno. Thus the procedure, which should have become an effective means of bridging the gap between micro- and macro-economic policy in fact became down graded to a supplementary instrument of regional policy.

Planning for the Eighties

If such shortcomings of *contrattazione programmatica* were yet to be revealed, it nevertheless was realized in the later 1960s that there was a need to move beyond the limited time horizon of five-year plans and ensure that medium-term planning was related to longer-term perspectives and horizons. This did not mean that planning had to be utopian. But in order to gain a perspective on feasible change, and to anticipate anything approaching a fundamental change in the structure of an economy, one has to have a planning horizon of at least ten and preferably fifteen years. Certainly one needs a fifteen-year dimension in order to try to re-shape final demand patterns and income distribution, land use, technologies, and the quality of life.

It was for such reasons that, in the late 1960s, we began to think in and for the longer term. The result was a report known as Project for the Eighties – *Progetto Ottanta*.[7] This was not a plan as such. But it created a framework for reasoning in the long term that could have provided the basis for specific medium-term planning measures. In a sense the process of drawing up the Project for the Eighties was the high season of postwar Italian planning. It represented the best in the planning effort, and not least because it meant a chance to change the future rather than simply projecting it. This was illustrated, in particular, by the inclusion for the first time of land use planning into the general perspectives for the national economy as a whole.

In 1970–1 we started drawing up the second five-year plan in Italy, using the long-term perspectives of the Project for the Eighties.[8] There were several innovations. One was the incorporation of what we called a Project Framework – *Progetto Quadro*. This represented a method of trying to quantify and spell out for an initial five years the implications of structural and social change specified as targets by the perspective for the eighties. This Project Framework involved construction of a reference framework of highly disaggregated socio-economic accounts, including indicators of the quality of life and standard of living. I return to these, and to its method of analysis, later in this chapter.

The second five-year plan was supposed to cover the 1971–5 period. However, the political situation in Italy at the time, with increasing strains and ultimate breakdown of the Centre-Left coalition, undermined the feasibility of any long-term planning view. The change created a divergence of views within the group of planners concerned in the Project Framework. Some of them believed that the best way to respond to the political situation was to challenge both politicians and administrators with claims of feasibility for precise targets related to the overall performance of the system. Others wanted to be more realistic, avoiding an overall planning approach and opting for practical projects at the sectoral and local levels.

In practice, both groups failed. The second Italian five-year plan was never endorsed in official form. For one thing, like the first plan, it was delayed, but this time for a longer time – from 1971–5 to 1973–7. More importantly, even this postponed form of the plan failed to secure government approval and adoption. It has been published by the Institute of Planning, the official institute dependent on the Ministry of the Budget and Economic Planning, but purely as a study. With the change in the overall political situation in the later 1970s, there clearly also are new prospects for planning. But if they are to be realized, they will need not only the force of political support, but also a clear understanding of what can be meant by socialist rather than capitalist planning.

Towards Socialist Planning

Why 'socialist' planning? What, in fact, can it mean? To date, its meaningfulness is due more to the historical and political experience of planning rather than to the elaboration of a methodology for socialist planning as such. The description of planning as 'socialist' in general reflects more the wish to emphasize a political choice in contrast with capitalist planning than a different way of proceeding, or a different technique, for planning itself. In other terms, the description of planning as 'socialist' shows a greater divergence from capitalist planning in terms of objectives or ends than a divergence of methods and techniques for managing society.

For these reasons many people think of planning in terms of instruments to rationalize choices – choices which themselves have been made outside the planning process itself. Of course, one has to recognize that different objectives can indeed be taken to distinguish socialist from capitalist planning. These include, for instance, equality of opportunity, better distribution of income, an emphasis on social and collective services, and so on.

However, beyond this, socialist planning is really different from capitalist planning in another respect: it is a new methodology for planning itself. To be socialist, planning must innovate both new criteria and new means for calculation, new means for utilizing data and, overall, the relationships between data. This paper is dedicated to this kind of innovation, in however synthetic a way.

The operating principles of the capitalist productive system – as theorized by economics as a 'science' – for a long time have obliged many contemporary industrial societies to adopt new methods of making economic policy. Why? To overcome the irrationality or entropy of the growth mechanism (cyclical fluctuations, unemployment, waste, inflation, imbalance – both geographical and social – congestion, poverty, and so on) with certain 'feedback' mechanisms.

In this way we have hypothesized, and sometimes also implemented, a kind of economic planning that, simulating the operating principles of the capitalist productive system, could optimize the relationship between goals and constraints with the help of specific policy instruments (e.g. taxation level, rate of interest, public investment, and so on).

But in this way, as well, the operating principles of such planning have kept the operating principles of the capitalist system. And this means a perception of social reality from the viewpoint and with the economic categories of the capitalist system – categories which, up to now, have been the indicators of welfare economics and the success of the productive system: e.g. production (GNP), productivity, employment, profits, wages, prices, capital and its accumulation, consumption, investment, and savings.

But increasingly, this question is being posed: are such indicators a good 'proxy' for social reality and of social welfare? Or are we still caught in the fetishism of GNP, i.e., the new macro form of what Marx called fetishism of commodities? Are we not caught in the mystification of 'exchange value' which, as is well known, has generalized and hegemonized production relations which are typical of the capitalist market?

It is increasingly credible and feasible to distinguish socialist planning substantially from capitalist planning. But to do so we must perceive and conceptualize social reality from a different viewpoint and with other categories. These categories are the indicators of *real* social needs, and not those needs used by the mystification of exchange value and the fetishism of commodities. To perceive social reality in socialist terms we need 'socialist indicators,' or more simply social indicators that could express welfare in terms of changed social allocation and social relationships. Or, in other words, from the indicators by which welfare is expressed as needs *to be* satisfied. This is why the indicator of social welfare is also a 'planning indicator' or 'action indicator,' i.e. a 'decision indicator.'

So a key problem for socialist planning is to rank and trade off individual preferences and collective preferences expressed in terms of social welfare or planning indicators. In the case of individual preferences the traditional market mechanism could be an adequate tool, subject to the key condition that people could manifest preferences in a situation of income equality, of accessibility to the goods and services of the market, and equality of information. As far as such conditions can be realized in certain ways (for instance by political action or by chance) the free agency of individuals on the market can still constitute an efficient tool for determining the sum of individual preferences, and for maintaining or promoting the productive mechanism.

As far as such conditions are not realized in practice, one can hypothesize other methods to surrogate 'the market': for instance, market research not only in the sample sense but in the voting sense (i.e., 'market polls'). In this way we can ensure a response which equalizes otherwise unequal conditions (income, education, etc.). In the case of collective preferences, concerning either social welfare or individual goods and services for whatever final use on which the community expresses its judgement, the ranking and the trade-off is a responsibility of the political authorities. There is no real problem here, from the methodological viewpoint, in organizing an optimal choice in terms of techniques of decision-making (cooperation between planners and politicians) – Planning, Programming, and Budgeting systems, etc., are one such example.

To implement the trade-off between different objectives and

satisfaction of wants (and to that end, different resource and consumption aims), socialist planning must both be wide-ranging and give importance to the political role in goal formulation and determination. It must involve the largest possible participation of parliaments as well as individuals and intermediate institutions in society, including the trade unions.

In other terms, socialist planning must not only involve but also entirely condition the activity of the main political bodies in society, i.e., the representative institutions at national, regional, and other levels. More specifically, procedures and institutions must be shaped *in terms of* the planning process. In this way planning must be central and peripheral – both primary and secondary.

In capitalist planning the process concerned is viewed mainly as *technical*, performed by the executive authorities and, in many cases, by technical bodies of this executive. In socialist planning, the representative political bodies must themselves perform the planning process. It is from the process of planning itself that the political institutions should reclaim their *raison d'être*, and should be reinvested with both the role and prestige that they have lost with the degeneration and sterilization of 'parliamentarism'.

The Feasible Transition

The transition from capitalism to socialism, from this overall viewpoint, means the progressive introduction of planning methods with socialist indicators into the process of society's 'self-management'. And this in turn would be related to the progressive introduction of new means for optimizing choices with reference to these socialist indicators – either directly or by successive stages.

Overall, therefore, socialist planning can be progressively introduced in the European countries which are still characterized by capitalist production only if and to the extent that they transcend the use of conventional judgements in quantitative terms. Further, socialist planning – as a process of political negotiation – should establish new targets which express the physical and financial accounting of interrelated and comparable social objectives. A new system of accounting the costs and benefits of society could reveal the inconsistencies between the traditional indicators and the new social objectives. And thus it could reveal the manner in which the productive mechanism must be transformed in order to realize those objectives that have been established in terms of the new indicators.

However, if socialist planning can be introduced progressively, this is not to say that it can be merely empiricist, incremental, or gradualist. In fact, it must be rationally *de*ductive. In other words, it must hypothesize a future state or situation identified in terms of social indicators. And from this situation it must reconstruct the present state or situation in terms of the same indicators. It is only at this point that a comparison should be made of the present situation, perceived in terms of planning indicators, and the conventional indicators of the capitalist productive system.

In principle such a system would reveal those present mechanisms which can – or cannot – be considered sufficient for the projection of conditions for the future state. The functional differences between the two systems – capitalist and socialist – are such that it is highly probable that the present mechanisms would be found almost wholly inadequate for the new aims. But to the extent that the contrast between present and future (old and new) is not undertaken, there will be no sound basis for judgement. The models which express the relationship between the indicators of the two different situations are parametric – that is, expressed as stable and fixed coefficients. But if the comparison changes the relationship, the parameters themselves then must be changed. This is the reason why the models expressing the present reality cannot be used for socialist planning.

The rational-deductive method of defining the future state of affairs and of regressing to the present situation does not mean, as some people think, ignoring the concept of planning-as-a-process, i.e., planning as a continuous adaptation of a situation. It means only denying that this adaptation is possible by using a model which has been constructed on the base of the present situation. To reconcile the concept of planning as a means of deducing the future state with the concept of planning as a process, we must introduce a *permanent confrontation* between the present and future indicators.

For instance, capitalist planning can be defined as assuming what the systems analysts call the 'analogism', or in other terms the process of simulating reality, as point of departure for the formulation of ends and objectives – a formulation which is itself an intermediate step in the planning process. Such simulation of reality is considered as something in which social phenomena are viewed as an open system. That is, unlike the physical sciences in which an experiment can be undertaken time and time again, the process of experiment is 'unrepeatable'.

Socialist planning, by contrast, applies normative criteria, not abstracted from the present reality, and contrasts these criteria with reality, attempting to make feasible a process of transition from the present constraints to the future norms or objectives. In this sense, socialist planning is a process of continuous experiment.

Transition in Perspective

If we consider the historical experience of socialist planning in terms of the previous considerations, we can manage a better explanation of the failure of such planning in many cases.

The major failure is that of the so-called socialist countries. The fact is that these countries have considered planning as a transformation of the productive system only in an institutional sense (collective appropriation, etc.). The operating principles of capitalist planning have been maintained, albeit under state ownership of the means of production, distribution, and exchange. Thus capitalist planning has been undertaken in the form of *state* capitalist planning. Everyone knows that there has recently been a major debate – including the so-called socialist countries – aimed at improving and democratizing the decision-making process. But it is only when a process of social negotiation of new options, ends and targets is introduced into the planning of these countries, including the future state of socialism itself, that one will have a real transition from state capitalist planning to socialist planning. This is not to say that the existence of the 'institutional' reforms, such as appropriation of the means of production, etc., will not facilitate the kind of transition which we have described.

However, our main concern is the Western countries. Despite the recuperative capacity of the capitalist system, which has been able to recover and sustain itself through the enlargement of 'new frontiers' in scientific and and technological terms, it seems clear that we live in a time of irreversible crisis in which the main problems of the past have been concentrated. It cannot be said that capitalist countries have not tried some form of economic planning. But the weakness of all such experience of planning in these countries, if we take the point of view developed earlier in this chapter, lies in the fact that the capitalist planning process no longer is technically possible inasmuch as it projects into the future a past which in fact is unrepeatable. Social and political demands are expressed in terms of real needs (social factors, quality of life, environment, etc.) which do not correspond to the dominant economic categories of the present productive system on which capitalist planning assumes to build the future. Thus, unless there is a reconstruction of the system of evaluation of objectives, and a new social accounting framework, there cannot be any application of appropriate categories for an effective form of planning. In other words, the European countries either will achieve a socialist planning in these senses we have already described, or will not plan at all.

The case of Italy is symptomatic. Italy is half capitalist and half pre-capitalist, half private and half state-owned, with a high concentration of capital both productive and financial – an ideal country for transition to socialism and planning. The fact that planning has effectively failed in Italy is partly due to the fact that it was an attempt at capitalist planning in a country in which capitalist relations were already in large part transcended. One has to make the leap, courageously, beyond mature capitalism, rather than reproduce the mechanisms of the past.

Thus the feasibility of socialist planning depends on both new values and criteria for social welfare, as well as institutional reform of the productive system. Any reform of this productive system which was not first characterized by clarification of the final purposes of society, i.e., final consumption, aims, and behaviour, would be crucially limited.

The institutional reform crucial to the problem is not just in the productive system itself, but at large – in the political system – reforming the constitutional function in our countries to allow the politically representative bodies to act as institutions for social planning.

We must expect to encounter tremendous difficulties in such reforms, country by country. Most probably these difficulties will be multiplied if we dream of transfer of such reforms to a European Community level. But it would be equally probable that such difficulties could be, in a certain sense, reduced by action at this level. Because we are constructing a European framework, maybe shaping a new order is easier than reform of an old order.

It depends mainly on the clarity of the ideas, methods, and action of the socialist movement and the wider Left in Europe, including the Communist parties. Whether we can transform the difficulties and the hopes for change into action and change itself depends on this wider Left.

Social and Qualitative Factors

Such clarity in ideas and action depends significantly on the extent to which socialist planning achieves a comprehensive framework for the allocation of resources on social rather than private criteria. This involves the integration of planning for new objectives with the specification of social and qualitative targets – in short, planning for welfare.

Much work has already been done in this field. There is, however, a dearth of clear methodological premises for the formulation of new social indicators; indeed, many of the difficulties encountered in this field of activity can be attributed to this deficiency.

Systematic efforts are now needed to construct a classification of those requirements that influence the quality of life. Only then will it be possible to suggest indicators appropriate for measuring those factors. Certainly an integrated approach encompassing the complete set of the factors is a major task.

Given its multidisciplinary character, such a task could hardly be handled by individual researchers working separately. Moreover, classification of the factors that influence quality of life requires choices that involve value-judgements. Even research groups with no official status have been hesitant to make or merely recommend such choices. This reticence and abdication of scholars, combined with indifference on the part of public agencies, has prevented adoption of any truly 'global' initiative in this field.

International public organizations, which are less involved in administrative routine than national governments, should be pressed to assume the burden of filling this vacuum. Trade unions should be encouraged to take part in the process. They should proceed, with expert backing, to the formulation of schema for classifying 'quality of life' factors in accordance with the social concepts and social goals of particular groups in society. In such a context, research on social indicators would be both more specific and more socially useful than isolated academic research.

As part of preparatory research for the drafting of medium term plans, the Italian government sponsored a first attempt at classifying those factors that determine the quality of life. The basis for such a classification was a specification of social objectives for all programmes involving use of national economic resources.

What was attempted was the construction of an overall 'system' attempting to specify those needs and goals deemed to be of collective interest. This 'system' – already described as Programme Structure (*Progetto Quadro*) – was represented by an interrelated sequence of four-digit items, in which each digit represented an 'end' for each succeeding number and a 'means' for each preceding number. These items were selected for their capacity to relate needs and the use of economic resources as already itemized in a system of national accounting.[9]

Italian experience suggests that such a structure can be used as a technique for integrating social accounts with a traditional economic accounting system.

Social accounts have often been founded on a system of 'social indicators' which are intended to measure – generally in physical terms – the costs and benefits of given levels of welfare. By remaining isolated from traditional economic accounts, this type of social accounting system has served a purely indicative function. It has been oriented towards an examination of current conditions and to the compilation of so-called 'social budgets' and 'social reports'. But it has not served an 'operational' function, nor been integrated with mainstream planning.

The Italian project integrated the two sets of accounts – both social and economic. The denominator common to both – or the bridge which links them – is final resource use. That is, 'social' goals need not be differentiated from 'economic' goals if we specify, as the common denominator, the resources which are necessary to achieve them.

The social accounting structure serves as a common classificatory schema both for determining the factors involved in the 'quality of life' and the sectors of final resource use arising out of the choices linked to goals, which are specified in the social accounts. Whatever may be the current availability of goods and services in each of the sectors of final use specified in the social accounts, modification of the current situation will imply a use of resources. That is to say that a certain absorption of resources is required for each step taken towards attainment of the 'standard' specified by a social indicator. Thus, in planning for future needs, a programmed accounting of resources may be obtained by integrating the items of traditional economic accounts with those of the social accounting structure.

In Italy this integration has been secured by constructing a two-part 'accounting framework' of resource use consisting of a current section and a programme-timed section. Each section has three dimensions: *sectoral*, in which resource use is disaggregated by sectors corresponding to the items of the programme-structure; *institutional*, in which the use is disaggregated by user institution (central and regional government, public agency, private and public enterprise, and family); and *geographical*, in which use is disaggregated by relevant territorial area (region and 'metropolitan system'). On the basis of this accounting framework by type of use, another has been constructed for formation or production of resources. The second framework has the same characteristics: two sections (current and programme-timed), and three dimensions (production by sector, by institution, and by geographical area).

The following tables indicate the kinds of criteria specified in the Italian exercise. Their effectiveness, as elsewhere in economic policy, depends on the political will behind their formulation, the range of views taken into consideration, and the pressure for their implementation in practice. Nevertheless, they illustrate that the priority given to social criteria in socialist planning can be incorporated in the planning framework itself.

Social accounting framework

AIM CATEGORY	DEFINITION OF THE LEVELS OF THE PROGRAMME STRUCTURE
1. PERSONAL SECURITY	
Activity directed to promote:	through an efficient system of:
1.1 Safeguards for the citizen and crime protection	1.1.1 Civil and penal legal activities
	1.1.2 Public security
	1.1.3 Special social work
1.2 Civil aid	1.2.1 Disaster aid
	1.2.2 Social emergency aid
1.3 Military defence	
2. PHYSICAL AND MENTAL WELL-BEING	
Activity directed to promote:	through an efficient system of:
2.1 Satisfactory life conditions	2.1.1 Food
	2.1.2 Other primary consumption
2.2 Health care provision	2.2.1 Overall health care
	2.2.2 Special health care
	2.2.3 In-patient hospital assistance
	2.2.4 Out-patient hospital assistance
	2.2.5 Drug and therapy prescription

3. WORK SATISFACTION

Activity directed to promote:

through an efficient system of:

3.1 Employment
- 3.1.1 Employment planning
- 3.1.2 Employment promotion
- 3.1.3 Employment security

3.2 Satisfactory work conditions
- 3.2.1 Trade-union associations
- 3.2.2 Worker conditions protection
- 3.2.3 Professional advancement
- 3.2.4 Protection against job accidents and on-the-job illness

3.3 Employment income
- 3.3.1 Income distribution
- 3.3.2 Protection against income reduction
- 3.3.3 Retirement

4. EDUCATION AND CULTURE

Activity directed to promote:

through an efficient system of:

4.1 Education
- 4.1.1. Elementary education
- 4.1.2 Secondary education
- 4.1.3 Advanced education
- 4.1.4 Permanent education

4.2 Culture and information
- 4.2.1 Cultural promotion
- 4.2.2 Enhancement of the cultural patrimony
- 4.2.3 Diffusion of culture and information
- 4.2.4 Cultural operations
- 4.2.5 Religious activities

5. RESEARCH AND INNOVATION

Activity directed to promote:

through an efficient system of:

5.1 Research
- 5.1.1 Basic research
- 5.1.2 Socially oriented research

5.2 Innovation
- 5.2.1 Technological innovation
- 5.2.2 Innovation in productive structures

6. LEISURE TIME AND RECREATION

Activity directed to promote:

through an efficient system of:

6.1 Sports activities
- 6.1.1 Individual and mass sports
- 6.1.2 Outdoor recreational activity

6.2 Touristic activities
- 6.2.1 Tourist facilities
- 6.2.2 Organization of tourism

6.3 Other recreational activities
- 6.3.1 Production of films, drama, etc., and intellectual recreation
- 6.3.2 Games

7. NATURAL ENVIRONMENT
   Activity directed to promote: through an efficient system of:
   7.1 Enhancement of the natural   7.1.1 Parks and natural reserves
       environment   7.1.2 Defence of the land and the
                                                   prevention of natural
                                                   catastrophes
                                             7.1.3 Control of pollution and
                                                   environmental problems
   7.2 Water production and use   7.2.1 Water production
                                             7.2.2 Water distribution

8. HOUSING AND URBAN ENVIRONMENT
   Activity directed to promote: through an efficient system of:
   8.1 Satisfactory housing conditions   8.1.1 Construction of new
                                                   residential units
                                             8.1.2 Re-adaptation, rehabili-
                                                   tation, and reorganization
                                                   of the housing stock
                                             8.1.3 Enhancement of historical
                                                   centres
                                             8.1.4 Acquisition of areas for
                                                   urbanization
   8.2 Access to housing   8.2.1 Rent policies
                                             8.2.2 Favourable conditions for
                                                   financing and credit
                                             8.2.3 Public housing

9 TRANSPORTATION AND
  COMMUNICATION
   Activity directed to promote: through an efficient system of:
   9.1 Urban transportation   9.1.1 Metropolitan railroad
                                                   communications
                                             9.1.2 Metropolitan street
                                                   communications
   9.2 National and international   9.2.1 National railroad
       transportation   communications
                                             9.2.2 National highway
                                                   communications
                                             9.2.3 Maritime communications
                                             9.2.4 Airway communications
   9.3 Special infrastructures for   9.3.1 Merchandise centres
       transportation of commercial   9.3.2 Energy pipelines
       goods
   9.4 Telecommunications   9.4.1 Postal and telegraphic
                                                   service
                                             9.4.2 Telephone, telex, and tele-
                                                   information services
                                             9.4.3 Radio-television

10. POLITICAL PARTICIPATION
Activity directed to promote: through an efficient system of:
10.1 Democratic participation   10.1.1 Political organization
                                                 10.1.2 Constitutional structure
                                                 10.1.3 Governmental
                                                         organization
                                                 10.1.4 National and territorial
                                                         economic and social
                                                         planning
                                                 10.1.5 Regional government
                                                         administration
                                                 10.1.6 Local government
                                                         administration

10.2 Participation, integration and   10.2.1 Participation in inter-
      international solidarity   national organizations
                                                         and communities
                                                 10.2.2 Bilateral international
                                                         relations

4

Project for Socialist Planning

Giorgio Ruffolo[1]

After twenty-five to thirty years of growth, the capitalist world has entered into a new and clearly difficult phase. The spectre of the 1930s has returned. Are we in the final stage of capitalism, too often announced and so often feared? Or are we faced with another of many cyclical crises? In reality, capitalism is a social system in continual crisis of transformation, with periods of slowing down and acceleration, and long cycles and brief fluctuations within them.

Economic Crisis

In the last century, as has been suggested by Ernest Mandel,[2] we can distinguish three major historial phases: the period of 'liberal capitalism,' from 1850 to 1895; the period of 'imperialist capitalism,' from 1895 to 1939; and the period of 'social capitalism,' or 'neo-capitalism,' from 1940 to the present. Each of these periods has included a qualitative transformation both of the techniques of production and of the relations of production; the so-called Industrial Revolutions were linked to a group of fundamental innovations – the steam motor, the electric motor, the electronic calculator. Each period can be divided broadly into two cycles of expansion and contraction (1850 to 1876, expansion, and 1876 to 1895, contraction; 1895 to 1914, expansion, 1914 to 1939, contraction). The third period, that of social capitalism, which began its expansionary phase at the end of the Second World War and continued into the 1960s, seems now to be entering into a phase of contraction.

The package of innovations which characterizes the third Industrial Revolution in three strategic sectors – electronics, atomic power and chemicals and their derivatives, underlies a gigantic increase in productive forces. Granted the institutions of postwar capitalism, and the relations of force between classes, these productive forces have been developed, with the support of the state, mainly by the large capitalist enterprises. These have appropriated the advantages of the new technologies, increasing their scale of production (and thereby their size and productivity). To the extent to which physical human energy has ceased to be the basis of production, large firms no longer derive profits simply from exploitation of the labour force. They are capable, thanks to the market power which their size assures, of gaining profits through their internal economies, incorporated in prices which they themselves fix.

The equilibrium wage of the system thus comes to be determined by the price and profit policies of big business. It varies in direct relation with productivity. It depends on the relations of force with the trade unions and with the extent to which the effective wage is inferior or superior to the equilibrium wage. In the former case there are depressive effects, and in the latter, inflationary effects in the system, granted the possibility for big business to determine prices.

Granted the unplanned nature of the system, the effective level of demand does not correspond necessarily to full employment. This is one of the reasons for intervention of the state through fiscal policy.

In this way, in the neo-capitalist system, trade unions can have a stabilizing role in the degree to which they accept effective wages relative to the level of equilibrium wages, and a de-stabilizing role in other respects. Government has a stabilizing role when public expenditure is managed effectively in relation to the full employment level, and a de-stabilizing role when it becomes an independent variable. The dynamic balance of the system therefore depends on certain relations of force between big business and other organized forces (state and unions) as

well as unorganized forces (smaller firms, consumers,
agricultural sector, etc.). It can well be claimed that from the end
of the Second World War to the end of the 1960s, such a
balanced development was guaranteed by the hegemony of big
business.

The political economy of the state served the interests of big
business far more than it disadvantaged them: guaranteeing a
certain level of aggregate demand, financing directly or
indirectly their investments, assuring them external economies,
and furnishing them with markets. Trade union pressure only
very rarely overcame the limits of a balanced wages growth. This
was principally a result in Italy of a relatively abundant labour
supply. Keynesian policies seemed to have resolved the
fundamental problems of the previous long cycle in capitalist
development, that of unemployment, apparently promoting a
virtuous circle of growth with stability. From the end of the
1960s, first on the international plane, and then secondly at the
level of particular national economies, this virtuous circle was
ruptured. The maintenance for several years of the level of
full employment and the saturation of essential consumer
demand introduced economic and political factors that de-
stabilized the system and introduced a vicious circle. The new
factors were crystallized in trade union power and political
power, in attaining the hegemony of big business and thus its
possibilities both for profit and for control of the system as a
whole.

Trade unions no longer limited themselves to exerting a
stimulus function on demand but took advantage of their
contractual power to impose wage demands which were
incompatible with the rules of the system, as well as normative
demands which transcended the economic field and both
contested and attacked the power of capitalism. State intervention became increasingly influenced by social forces and
was constrained to satisfy an economic demand for increasing
social services. Public expenditure thus became disfunctional
for the system, while limits and controls increasingly were
introduced over the action of business in general under the
pressure of a public opinion which became increasingly hostile
to the power of 'big business'.

There were two main features to the response of big business to this crisis. The first was an increase in their market power through concentration, which allowed them not only to reply to but actually to anticipate wage demands. This fuelled inflation. The second was the adoption of technologies and processes which save labour, restricting the outlets for the supply of labour, and thereby creating unemployment. In complement with this, big business tended to re-create a new reserve army of labour, either attracting categories of marginal (immigrant) labour or directing their investments towards countries where the labour market was more docile.

Political Crisis

This crisis of capitalism, as an economic and social system based on profit and unequal exchange, was parallelled by a crisis of the state as political system, which posed a threat to the future of democracy. During the last long phase of expansion, capitalism seemed to have found not only an economic but also a social and political balance in the new form of the welfare state, that is, the state of social capitalism. In place of a rigid distinction of political functions undertaken by the state and economic functions undertaken by the market, there arose a system of integrated command between big business, the political class, and the Civil Service administration. The economic success of such a system, capable of a growth which was practically uninterrupted in a quarter of a century, assured a certain relative social peace through the extension of a vast network of collective services and social security provisions, thereby allowing the maintenance and development of political democracy.

Today, the equation between economic growth, social welfare, and political democracy appears compromised. Social agitation preceded the economic crisis in Italy (1968, with its trade union demands, occurred during a period of full economic growth). One therefore has to seek the cause outside the market mechanism of capitalism itself. The crisis of our time had fundamentally political origins. Its specific character was an incompatibility between political demands and the institutions of capitalism. It is the development of these new political demands which can explain the fall in the rate of profit, and not the reverse.

In one sense, certainly, the new political demands were themselves a consequence of economic growth. The level of consciousness and information of a particular society depends on the level of its productive forces. But the inverse relationship, that is, the reaction between the super-structure and the sub-structure of the system, provides the key for an explanation of the current crisis. Specifically, economic growth generated new non-economic needs and the formation of social groups which demanded both recognition and powers of self-management within the capitalist system itself. These aspects of crisis came in addition to two fundamental ecological problems: the degradation of the environment, and an exponential growth in population. Of these two, the second is clearly the more critical. But in reality there is no hope of population control without a new distribution of resources. And this is not compatible with a capitalist framework.

The previous summary analysis does not allow any prediction of a particular outcome to the crisis based on 'the internal laws of movement' of history. It is true that the crisis of capitalism itself generates demands for a socialist alternative. But it does not thereby furnish the response to such demands. However, if it is clear that socialism does not build itself, it is important that the social forces in its favour are in a position to shape out in advance a model of society and a strategy which is coherent with socialism.

One of the typical aspects of the current crisis is the inefficiency of big units. The increase in size of businesses has been accompanied by centralization and bureaucratization, which has meant a disproportion between the upward and downward flows of information in the system. Its channels of information have been structured and framed in such a way as to guarantee a continuous flux of downward information (publicity, means of mass communication, entertainment, etc.) with only a weak flow of upward information (the political vote, consultation, the sounding out of opinion, etc.). It is this control of the channels of information that assures power to the big groups in the economy, to the political class, and to the bureaucracy. But this also thereby means their isolation from the rest of the system, granted the weakness of return information, or social reaction.

The apparatus of representative democracy, which should constitute the means for upward information through the entire system, is in crisis because it now represents an inadequate channel for the expression of rising political demands from the base. The problem of communication in an advanced social system, and a system of democratic planning, will be resolved neither through a further centralization of power, nor through its fragmentation into small units, but through the integration of small units in a decentralized framework. This implies a redistribution of power at various levels and their integration into the system of communication, which assures a continuous process of reciprocal adjustment of decisions taken at various levels.

The structure of such an organization could therefore be envisaged as a federated political system constituted by:

(a) the basic units, or 'micro democracy': local authorities, health authorities, education authorities, cultural associations and firms;
(b) more complex organizations, more 'sub systems', which constitute the higher grade of organization of the former units: regions, consortia of firms, regional and national sectoral associations;
(c) service organizations and information networks: hospital centres, data banks, big business, university centres, research centres;
(d) control and planning systems at the sectoral level (agencies);
(e) control and planning systems of central government.

Delegation, Negotiation, Arbitration

The relationships between the various levels should be regulated through representative *delegation*, *negotiation* and, in the last analysis, *arbitration* within the central system.

In order for such a system to work it must necessarily be planned. The organization of a democratic decentralized system with increased information and flexible response mechanisms implies a high grade of planning. Such a system would allow the development and extension of representative democracy through wide-ranging issues of a complex society. It also would allow the integration of forms of democracy and self-government at the base of the system.

Increased participation and direct democracy should not mean elimination of the function of authority within the system, but its insertion into a newly defined decision-making process: (a) in the definition of end; (b) in action and implementation; and (c) in control processes. The circuits of authority within the system cannot be the same as the circuits of control without blocking the system itself. Partly this confusion of circuits in 'governing democracy' has led to paralysis of the present system. Moreover, the function of control itself should be discontinuous.

Capitalist industrial societies and bureaucracies are founded on the principles of division and inequality, applied over the whole range of human life: in the division of *time*, of *work*, of *space*, of *wealth* and of *information*.

The relationship between the division of time and work is clear enough. Thus the day itself is divided between work on the one hand and 'free time' on the other. The fragmentation of time as a function of the work process shows its own irrationality when an increase in productivity in the system by saving 'productive labour' results in unemployment.

A society in which the organization of time will be reconstructed through the expressed cultural preferences of people themselves, constrained by necessary work, should obviously reduce the division of labour, and in particular the distinction between manual and intellectual labour, through obligatory social service and a rotation of jobs.

Equality, Information, and Response

A society in which necessary labour is a more equally distributed social responsibility could realize a more equal economic distribution of income, not related directly to individual productivity. Those who consider this a Utopian principle should reflect on the fact that today more than a quarter of so-called labour incomes in industrial society do not pass through the 'labour market' but are redistributed through administrative channels (state aids, subsidies, pensions, etc.).

In the current conditions of economic inequality and political democracy 'incomes policies' are utopian. The three elements are not compatible. Inequality and democracy generate chronic inflation. Inequality and incomes policy are fatal for democracy. A democratic incomes policy can only be egalitarian.

Capitalism disorganizes *space*, like time. It promotes the urban megalopolis and reduces the countryside to a desert. A socialist reorganization of space should be founded on a systematic synthesis of unity and diversity. Thus, as people's time should be reconstructed in line with their personalities, based on the diversity of the dimensions of work, of culture, of play, space should be reintegrated through the sovereignty of the citizen in the 'urban system'. The role of new channels of information and response is crucial in this respect for the urban and regional dimension of socialist planning, as in the other aspects already mentioned. In such a system natural parks, agricultural zones, industrial centres, commercial services, schools and universities, residential zones, recreation areas, etc., would combine the advantages of the small town with those of the big agglomerations while avoiding both isolation and congestion.

Planning is a specific form of integration of a democratic decentralized and egalitarian society. Where mechanisms of integration based on joint action and interaction are inadequate, the possible form of integration is a planning consensus on ends and means. The possibility of achieving such a consensus is related to the quality and distribution of information within society and to the efficiency of its communications structure.

Regulation and Organization

Contrary to technocratic opinion, decentralization, in a complex system, is the preliminary basis for integration.

The initiative for planning should neither start from above nor from below, but contemporaneously at all levels of decision-making giving rise to a simultaneous and continuous process of adjustment. The basic units, intermediate organizations, and national systems of government, each at its own level, should define their plan which would take the form of a message sent to the other units in the system, from which they receive information on return. The general plan and the continuous process of verification and adjustment that results from it should thereby be a two-way flow: one of *impulse* and the other of *regulation*.

Impulses are the decisions, programmes, and projects formed at all levels, from the individual to that of central government. Regulations take three forms: (a) immediate self-regulation; (b) contractual relations; (c) authoritative relations.

(a) *Self-regulation.* Already, in the area of the family, and in personal friendships, relations are not subject to a strict accountability. But other areas of relationship are limited by the capitalist market (which has reduced each relationship to one of purchase and sale); they also are limited by authoritarian relationships, which either constrain or manipulate behaviour, and thereby condition it. Socialist society, increasing the area of association, would thereby extend the area of direct relationships and self-regulation. In cooperative and other associations, in communes and communities, relationships between people could be developed without passing through the filter of the market.

(b) *Contractual relations.* In pre-capitalist mercantile societies the market did not imply the necessary exploitation of man by man. In a socialist industrial society this situation could be recreated at a higher level under conditions which did not imply the exploitation either of labour or of the consumer. The first is the reduction of automation. The second is the establishment of more balanced relationships between consumers and producers, through the reduction of consumer pressure such as advertising, and the establishment of wider ranging associations, communities, associated groups, etc., which could reresent a countervailing force to producers; also, in particular, through improved information. Therefore, a socialist society would not eliminate the regulation of the market, but would liberate it from monopolistic elements through decentralization and a new power balance between associations of producers and consumers. Such theoretical liberal conditions can only be made real through a democratic socialist order.

(c) *Authoritative relations*. The plans and decisions of each unit within the system should be subject to definite constraints from the higher system of planning within society. First, in urban planning, the regions would fix the constraints for the activity of local authorities and those of associations of individual citizens. Thus also at the macro-economic level, the national plan would pose the constraints for economic activity, which must be observed to assure coherence in the use and disposition of resources.

This requires, among other things, the adoption of a series of social *indicators* which translate the qualitative rulers of the game into quantitative constraints.

However, the accounting process for social indicators cannot be either merely technical nor technocratic. The determination of the indicators is a crucial and central factor in the planning process. They express political choices on the structural characteristics of society.

Moreover, the indicators must be considered not as technical parameters but as political variables, subject to collective social choice. Tensions will emerge through the planning process which must induce a continual review, verification, and rectification of the level and characteristics of the indicators.

Continual conflicts which arise during the process of planning therefore must be arbitrated through democratic decisions at a higher level. At the national level one can envisage a Planning Council which would represent the principal components of the system – large and small firms, trade unions, other associations, local authorities, etc. – and which was provided with both technical advice and a data bank.

At the highest level of social consciousness the plan would thus appear at the same time as (a) the process of regulating functions which society would undertake through new decentralized decision-making, and (b) as a process of impulse for the change which such new decisions and social projects would impart. It would be a *circular* and *continuous* process rather than a vertical imposition of priorities from above.

Project for Socialism

Such a process can be achieved only through a socialist transformation of the power relations in society, i.e., through a project or strategy for transition to socialism. Such a strategy must define a practical path towards socialism based on here and now: it has to base a projected future in the concrete present. This implies the acceptance of certain constraints at each phase of the process of transition. Alternative strategies of 'rupture' with the present as proposed by certain ultra-Left groups assume an ingenuous faith in the historical necessity of socialism.

The fundamental problems of such a strategy for transition to socialism relate to (a) the conditions for the achievement of power; (b) to the identification of those social groups which will support change, as well as (c) to the political programme for transition itself.

In relation to the first problem it is important to stress that there is an *asymmetry* in the question of power. The Left cannot take power in the same way as the Right. With the Right in power, the institutions within society continue to function for them. With the Left in power they cease to function for the government. As soon as the Left arrives in office the whole apparatus of the administration and the organization of the economy move out of reach and submerge out of sight. For this reason the Left must dispose of *its own power base*, in such a way as to be able to change – from the start – the shape and distribution of power in society without suffering an indefinite blackmail through paralysis of the system.

It is in such a context of the distribution of power that the strategy for new centres of decision-making and arbitration assume significance. Trade union organization is a formidable counter-power to capital, but is not sufficient in itself. It also is important to organize socialist counter-power within the economic system, in social institutions, in the educational system, in regional and local organizations, and in cultural life. It is not only a matter of achieving power in the sense of the conquest of what already is there, but also of *creating* new powers within a socialist society. Self-management and workers control clearly are key elements in this process. But the Left will achieve political power proper only when it has created a *critical mass* of its own support and pressure for change.

This means a strategy at two levels – both political and social. Politically, whether in opposition or in government, the parties of the Left must demand and contribute to structural reforms which pose the conditions for an enlargement of the socialist area in the economy: for example, major reforms in workers' rights, health, and education. At the social level they must pressure or act for change in the introduction of self-governing and self-managed institutions.

In relation to the question of the social groups which can support change, there is a major debate on the Left. A major problem in the debate lies in the incapacity of some of the Left to recognize the difference between the reality of social classes today and the inherited conceptual framework from the past. A polarized class analysis, based on *bourgeoisie* and proletariat, is manifestly inadequate as an interpretation of the complex social structure of advanced industrial society. This is not only because of the general importance of a 'new middle class' emerging alongside a tenaciously persistent old middle class, or because of a process of differentiation within the working class and the *bourgeoisie*. It is important also because there are new differences quite apart from class as determined by the place of different groups in the productive process. There is the difference of generations (the new role of the young); of sex (the new role of feminism); and new dimensions to status in key professions (intellectuals, and researchers, etc.).

Any socialist strategy seriously in the business of mobilizing support must be based on an analysis of class and social structure which admits not only classes but also social strata, cultural conditions, and specific social situations in relation to the power of modern capitalism. It is only in such a way that it will be possible to identify the *basic potential coalition* of forces for socialism.

This is a matter of a potential coalition in the sense that only a political and educational programme, related to actual struggle, experiment, persuasion, and pressure can translate the opposition within capitalism of women, ethnic groups, students, the young, and others into a conscious challenge to capitalism (in Marxist terms, the difference between coalition *in* itself to coalition *for* itself).

These two fundamental problems of transition for socialism – (a) the realization of a basic potential coalition of forces and (b) the implementation of a working coalition between temporary alliances and basic social forces – can countervail the hegemony of capitalist and bureaucratic élites only if they are integrated into a democratic programme. It is in this sense that they are both a necessary condition for transition to socialism, and dependent on a programme, strategy, and planning framework which can organize a socialist project for society.

The extension of such an alliance, its content, and the rate of progress of the programme for change clearly cannot be based on abstract criteria, but must be related to the specific historical situation. In contemporary Italy this demands a particular flexibility not only in planning, but also in the politics of alliance on the Left.

It is for such reasons that the basic potential coalition of forces can only be based on the unity of the Italian Left. The present divisions between parties and movements of the Left in Italy are at the same time ideological, traditional, and practical. Today, no one could credibly argue that there are major differences among the *aims* of the main parties of the Left. The divisions of the Left both in Italy and abroad relate mainly to the inertia of existing institutions and past attitudes. No one, similarly, could deny the reality of such divisions. It is in this context that the concept of a project for a new society, related to new processes for the distribution and exercise of power, plays a key role. Only such a democratic project can provide the conditions on which a new coalition of forces can promote a new hegemony within the economy and society.

PART III

German Perspectives

5

The 'Social Market' in Crisis

Karl Georg Zinn

For many people, the recent problems of economic development in the Federal Republic of Germany seem to have been caused by the world-depression beginning in 1973, and especially by the increase in oil-prices. Economically the timing of the oil-price increase coincided with the beginning of the depression. Politically, it could be explained as the consequence of a decline in imperialist power and the political failure of Western countries to deploy an acceptable framework of development for the poor countries during the last thirty years.

But one might ask whether the timing of the oil price increases was accidental. There were other connections between the impact of the OPEC cartel and the growing economic difficulties of the capitalist states. Certainly, the oil-price increase does not explain the deeper causes of the current depression. Indeed, there is evidence that the rise of oil prices even pushed up investment which otherwise would not have been undertaken.

To understand the current crisis in the West German economy, we have to look more closely at the postwar development of the capitalist countries themselves.

The German situation looks comparatively better than that of most of her neighbour countries, though, as will be shown, the well-known result of a harsh deflationary policy – higher unemployment – is true for Germany in a classic way – if the veil of statistical sorcery is lifted. Nevertheless, the German economy seems to be pretty strong, especially if we use international balance of payments comparisons as a criterion; the strength of exports grew during the thirty years of German postwar economic history. But to understand the story of Germany's success on foreign markets we have to look back to the beginning of the so-called *Wirtschaftswunder*.

There were three main factors of the long-term economic development of postwar Germany.[1] First, an abundance of highly skilled labour. Second, an absence of under-consumption or realization problems (a) because of the long-lasting undervaluation of the currency and (b) as in other countries – the guarantee of a fast recovery in domestic consumption because of suppressed demand during the war. Third, as a corollary, a rapid accumulation fostered not only by the low wage level, which was the complement of labour abundance, but also by several public schemes for capital formation, such as tax relief for retained profits on all kinds of investment grants.

During the years from 1950 until 1966 the key factor in the process of stabilization was the role of the central bank, the *Deutsche Bundesbank*. The fact that the German central bank – compared to other countries – has a completely independent position is frequently overlooked. The government has neither the right nor the practical ability to force the central bank to execute monetary measures. Though it can influence the personnel of the central bank's policy board, the *Zentralbankrat*, which has thus become more and more a political instead of an expert body, the central bank has followed its own path. This has often led in a different direction from government policy because of the different priorities of the two institutions: the central bank believed itself to be obliged mainly to stabilize the price level, even if this created unemployment.

Governments were frequently opposed to the central bank – mostly in vain. Until now, however, the critics of the central bank's independence from government and parliamentary control could not pass any bill to change the bank's undemocratic powers. Generally it is still purported that the independence of the central bank – often characterized as a fourth power along with parliament, the judiciary, and government – is a necessary condition for a neutral monetary policy. This, of course, is a consequence of neo-liberal ideology, which follows the fiction of a neutral state and the theoretical separation of public politics and private capitalist economics.

The independence of the German central bank did not of course extend to the exchange rate. In practice, until the breakdown of the Bretton Woods fixed rates system, international capital flows mostly defeated domestic monetary policy, either at once or when tight money at home became self-defeating because of an increasing export surplus and the equivalent imported inflation. The strong position of the central bank was one reason for the lack of coordination of government and central bank measures during several years. The most important examples were the tight money policies of 1966 and 1973–4, when the accidental counterbalancing of fiscal and monetary policy contributed to failures of stabilization policy.

The Reserve Army of Labour

The economic difficulties which the Federal Republic experienced during the recession of 1967–8 and during the recent depression since 1973 might seem to be relatively harmless compared to the rates of unemployment and inflation in her neighbour countries. But this is only partly true for unemployment because of Germany's policy to sweep out more than 600,000 migrant labourers between September 1973 and December 1975, which thereby reduced the registered number of unemployed. The reduction of the migrant labour force during the recession of 1967–8 also pulled down the apparent rate of unemployment in the same way. The decrease in the number of migrant workers at this time was around 230,000, i.e., 18·5 per cent of the foreign labour force. To underline the point, the migrant labourers which return to their home countries are not included in the published number of German unemployed.

It seems doubtful if the German governments in 1965–6 and 1973 would have been inclined to pursue their anti-inflationary policy of sudden tight money and budget cuts on such a scale if they could not have relied upon such an enormous reduction in relative unemployment by a parallel reduction of migrant labour. At least the deflationary measures started in December

1973 and continued during 1974 would have been much more harmful if the acceleration of redundancies had not been counterbalanced by a reflux of foreign workers to Turkey, Greece, etc. A weaker anti-inflationary policy in 1973, and a stronger Keynesian approach in demand management, could have kept the rate of inflation on its original level of seven per cent or thereabouts. But fiscal and monetary policy during the years 1974–5, though not without anti-cyclical effects, was successful only in so far as the rate of unemployment appeared to be stopped and sank then slowly because of the buffer effect of the dismissed reserve army of foreign workers. The achievement of a sinking cost-of-living index and relatively low inflation, with the government's ability to present the outcome as the result of a well-balanced fine-tuning exercise, has to be seen in connection with this handling of labour-power.

However, the use of foreign labour was not merely cosmetic. It also was central to the rapid expansion of the postwar Germany economy. The explanation of the West German *Wirtschaftswunder* is mainly given by the fact that during the 1950s there was a continous replenishment of the reservoir of highly skilled labour by more than two million persons coming from the German Democratic Republic; during the sixties the suction of foreign labour began. Both facts explain why there was no lack of relatively cheap labour, which is one of the most important conditions for accumulation.

But how was postwar Germany able to absorb such a growing number of workers? Who bought the growing mass of commodities produced by them? The answer is twofold. First, the undervaluation of the currency opened the world market from the beginning of the new post-war German state. From 1951 until now there has been no single year with an adverse balance of visible trade, and the current balance only twice showed a deficit – because of payments by migrant workers to their home countries. Secondly, as previously mentioned, the domestic market expanded rapidly because of suppressed demand due to the war. Export demand and domestic consumption induced further demand for capital formation. As long as management could be sure that there would be no realization problem, there was a high propensity to invest. The financing of the high rate of capital formation was pretty easy: low wages, grants and subsidies for investment, and tax relief for retained profits.

Accumulation and Crisis

During the 'accumulation years', especially 1950 to 1960, the standard of living in West Germany had of course been below that of other industrialized Western countries. But this was not generally recognized by the German people, and even if they had grasped that the average propensity to consume stayed below that of Great Britain or the United States, it would have been accepted as self-evident for a defeated society which was striving to wipe out the political and economic mortgage of the fascist period.

Moreover, the social and economic reference model proper was the 'other' Germany beyond the Iron Curtain. And, indeed, this comparison was very flattering for the Western part of the nation. Basically, economic conditions of development and accumulation during the immediate postwar period mostly favoured the Federal Republic: for instance, no reparations; whereas East Germany lost almost $30 billions up to 1953 by the dismantling of plant and other reparations in kind. During this period Marshall aid flooded into the Western countries, including West Germany. Also, East Germany lost Silesia through border changes; thus the German Democratic Republic lost its industrial base in coal and steel. The political differences and the growing discrepancy in standard of living between the two German states caused the long stream of refugees from East to West. This brought a further shift in the development of both states: upwards for the West with a skilled labour gain; downwards for the East with a skilled labour loss.

The capital accumulation of West Germany thus was based upon a historic combination of an inflow of highly skilled labour, and a re-built infrastructure, which had been destroyed during the war mainly in housing, schools, universities, nursing homes, etc. Production-oriented transport facilities either were less destroyed or quickly repaired to prevent severe bottleneck-effects. Also there was no profit realization problem. Medium- and long-term investment expectations were highly optimistic, because almost everything that could be produced was sold – on the domestic or foreign markets. It is well known that optimistic expectations of companies lead to an acceleration of investment and national income – as long as the whole system procures enough reaffirmation that investment expectations are correctly set. In such a favourable situation the normal business cycle and its troughs do not interrupt the medium-term trend of growth, but produce only some retardation during recessions.

But capitalist accumulation defeats itself as soon as the expansion of markets begins to slacken – the accelerator principle now works downwards. The overall shape of development changes its direction: the upward trend is reversed in a downward direction; the business cycle shows peaks which are becoming shorter and less powerful, the troughs are longer and deeper – and continuing rationalization raises structural unemployment.

Structural unemployment is increasingly characteristic of contemporary West German industry.[2] The situation is combined with growing problems within the education system: the unemployment of school-leavers because of a lack of apprenticeships has increased above average; the same situation is found within the group of young academics who want to start their professional employment. Medium-term rates of growth of capital formation are declining, and the average vintage of capital has been growing since the beginning of the seventies. Efforts for rationalization of capital are intensified; the proportion of investment allocated to rationalization is growing steeply, whereas capital widening is declining. The corollary is evident: destruction of jobs instead of creation of new jobs.

It may be questioned whether the 'investment-gap' since 1970 amounts to 160 billion Deutschmarks, or is less. But the main long-term indicator for the development of the economy, the rate of capital growth, as illustrated by the following figures, shows clearly that the 'Wirtschaftswunder' has gone.

Rates of growth of gross capital formation/average p.a.

1950/54	1955/59	1960/64	1965/69	1970/74
9·2%	7·1%	6·3%	3·0%	0·2%

Source: W. Glastetter, *Die wirtschaftliche Entwicklung der Bundesrepublik Deutschland im Zeitraum 1950 bis 1975*, in: Industriegewerkschaft Metall, *Materialien zur Tagung Krise und Reform in der Industriegesellschaft*, Frankfurt/M 1976, p. 69.

The long-term development of capital formation, which was induced by strong domestic and foreign demand and fostered by the plethora of skilled labour (which still exists), now shows declining growth and stagnating demand respectively. The gap between disposable income and household expenditures gets wider, and the propensity to save grows correspondingly. This deployment of a stagnating consumption has to be seen against the background of German households' traditionally low propensity to consume. During the 1970 boom the Germans spent 54·2 per cent of their national income on private consumption; the equivalent figures for the United Kingdom are 61·6 per cent, for France 58·8 per cent, for the United States 61·2 per cent, and for Japan 50·3 per cent.[3] It is no coincidence that Japan and Germany, the two leading export-countries within OECD, show the lowest private consumption as a share of national income. The growth of purchasing power of their population, though absolutely high, stayed behind the growth of national income.

Thus the absorption of these economies was too low to equilibrate their balance of payments. The repeated revaluations and appreciations of their currencies were corollaries of a relative lack of domestic demand. The inflationary process within these countries had mainly been caused by imported inflation. There is nothing exciting about the fact that generally retarded and very moderate revaluations did not change the upward trend of exports, nor the structure of exporting industries. The revaluations were forced reactions, not measures to prevent the continuing inflow of inflation from world markets.

Of course undervaluation of a currency does not itself explain why a country keeps a strong position on the world market.

There are many other important factors, such as deliveries on time, after-sales-service, and in general a supply tailored to customers' needs abroad. But these factors are deployed by feedback during the long-term apprenticeship of an exporting country. The more interesting question is how to become an exporting country, i.e., how to get into position rather than how to keep it. A country which, like Germany, has built up a dominant export sector and thus is heavily dependent on further exports gets a bias in favour of export industries. The whole economic policy, including the foreign exchange rate, is bound to pay special regard to the needs of exporting companies. The contradictions between domestic anti-inflationary policy and lagged revaluations, the 'tight wage' policy, the country's insufficient absorption of surpluses on the current balance, and above all the growing dependence of domestic employment on a world market whose demand is partly financed by the country itself, all corroborate that bias.

Looking back into the development of pre-war Germany many people think that the *Wirtschaftswunder* had mainly been the consequence of the neo-liberal concept of a 'social market' economy. This expression does not hide more than the belief that the competitive market creates growth, efficiency, and an overall equilibrium, but lacks social justice. The former has to be protected against monopolies and cartels by a competiton policy; the latter needs some special arrangements for labour markets and a more or less comprehensive system of public insurance (health service, retirement payments, etc.).

The social insurance system had been built up to a comparatively high standard before the war. The most important postwar achievement was the so-called dynamization of retirement payments, which can briefly be explained as an anti-cyclical, index-linked system: the retirement-payments are accounted on the base of the average income level of the insured population three years ago. This system can be based upon self-financing as long as there is no severe and long-lasting slump, and so long as there is no sharp decline of employed people or an increase of those who get retirement payments. Lately the system has needed more and more subsidies from the taxpayers.

The second buttress of the 'social market' economy, or more

exactly of its theory, is the salient meaning given to the competition policy. Indeed there is a long story of postwar German competition policy, a story which begins with ten years' delay in introducing a Monopolies Act, the *Gesetz gegen Wettbewerbsbeschränkungen (Kartellgesetz)*. Ludwig Ehrhard, the political promoter of the social market economy, tried in vain to establish a tough anti-monopoly policy at the beginning of the economic development of the Federal Republic. The industrial lobby was against it. Thus a watered-down bill passed parliament only on 27 July 1957. The crucial test was whether the basic principle forbade cartels and monopolies, or only sought to prevent misdemeanours to the rules of workable competition. The weaker principle survived. In general there was no effective control against concentration until the late 1960s. An amendment to the cartel law in 1973 gave the possibility to control mergers in advance, i.e., they have to be approved by the Federal cartel office.

Marginal effects aside, competition policy played no important role for the accumulation and growth of the German economy. Possibly expansion would in fact have been less dynamic if strong brakes had been put on the concentration process. In particular, export markets were gained mainly by big business, save for one important exception – the machine tool industry.

Export Dependence

The advantage of the German exporting industries on world markets had been established during the first ten to fifteen years after the formation of the new German postwar state. As with Japan's exporting power, the drive was given by the adaptation of high technology. The premise was a high rate of accumulation and a continuous modernization of industry. We have demonstrated that these conditions characterized postwar German development. Visible exports have been concentrated upon investment goods and the products of chemical, scientific, and related industries. The ratio of primary production to visible exports did not exceed 7 per cent of total visible exports until 1975. The balance of invisible trade has mostly been adverse since 1965; i.e., Germany is a commodity exporter, not a servicing country. The relation of visible to invisible trade is roughly four to one.

Visible exports: Germany

Year	Total %	Primary industry, food and tobacco	Investment goods	Materials for Industry	Consumer goods	Sundries
1965	100	6·6%		26·9%	10·5%	1·6%
1966	100	5·8%	54·4%	27·4%	10·6%	1·7%
1967	100	5·9%	53·3%	26·5%	10·6%	1·6%
1970	100	6·0%	54·2%	27·0%	11·2%	1·6%
1973	100	6·7%	53·9%	26·5%	11·6%	1·3%
1974	100	6·9%				1·3%
1975	100	7·6%	53·3%	27·5%	10·3%	1·8%

Source: *Statistische Beihefte zu den Monatsberichten der Deutschen Bundesbank*, Reihe 3: *Zahlungsbilanzstatistik*, October 1976, p. 2b.

Because of the comparatively low elasticity of demand for German investment equipment, repeated revaluations and appreciations did not stop the growth of visible exports but only reduced rates of export growth temporarily.

It has already been mentioned that the revaluations of the Deutschmark have to be seen as reactions to an increase of the price level of world markets. Until the late sixties, when world inflation began to accelerate, there was only one pretty modest revaluation of the Deutschmark – on 3 June 1961 – with a 5 per cent increase of the exchange rate; from 9 September 1949 until that date there was no German revaluation at all. The next revaluation was on 10 October 1969, with a 9·3 per cent increase. The following years then brought a series of revaluations and appreciations of the currency, as shown in the following table.

Floating rates are only a *conditio sine qua non* for successive appreciation of exchange rates for a country with permanent surplus in the current balance. But the appreciation might be counterbalanced by capital outflow. This happened in 1974, the

Year	Rate of growth of visible exports	Date of revaluation	Per cent revaluation	$ price
1966	12·52%			
1967	7·95%			
1968	14·36%			
1969	14·07%	27/10/1969	9·3%	3,6600
1970	10·31%			
1971	8·56%	21/12/1971	13·6%	3,2225
1972	9·56%			
1973	19·71%	14/2/1973 19/3/1973 (float)	11·1%	2,9003
1974	29·25%	average p.a.	2·6%	2,5897
1975	−3·89%	average p.a.	4·9%	2,4631

Source: Statistische Beihefte zu den Monatsberichten der Beutschen Bundesbank,
Reihe 3: *Zahlungsbilanzstatistik,* October 1976, pp. 2b, 18a, 18b and
computations by the author.

year with the highest surplus of visible exports (over 50 billion
Deutschmarks) when the deficit on the capital balance reached
24 billion Deutschmarks; in 1975 there was again a deficit on the
capital balance (11 billion Deutschmarks). Thus the
appreciation of the German exchange rate during the years 1974
and 1975 did not correctly reflect the high surplus on the current
balance.

Summarizing the main points, it should be clear that German
exports depend upon the difference between domestic and
international inflation, and the lagged appreciation of the
German currency. The domestic anti-inflationary policy of
German governments was successful, and this policy produced a
competitive advantage as a by-product. It also should be clear
that German export strength was built upon: (a) an abundance
of skilled and comparatively cheap labour; (b) fast capital
accumulation during the first ten to fifteen years of the Federal
Republic; (c) a long-lasting undervaluation of the German
currency; (d) a permanent difference between German and
international inflation rates and a lagged reaction of German
appreciations to the international inflationary process (because
of domestic anti-inflationary measures which reduced German
employment, but which because of emigrant labourers did not
proportionally push up the unemployment rate); (e) an extreme

dependence of German employment on exports, promoting a political bias in favour of exporting industries.

Thus the threatening problem of structural unemployment is mainly a question of the future development of world market trends. It seems obvious that Germany has maintained her full employment level only by permanent surpluses on current balance – and reverse deficits in other countries. Thus Germany's interest in solving the balance of paymentsproblems of her main customers is not so altruistic. But it is difficult to regain full employment while reducing the high dependence on foreign trade, especially if deficit countries such as Britain and Italy move into surplus, which they must do if they are to redeem their international loans, and which Britain appears set to do thanks to North Sea oil.

Thus Germany needs a deliberate policy of structural change. Self-regulation by market mechanisms led the country into its position as an exporter with permanent surpluses on the current balance, i.e., a country, which owes part of its full employment to deficits in other economies. Consequently the necessary structural change for the German economy also severely concerns the employment problem of other countries. It might be that full employment policy has to be based in future mainly upon domestic measures and cannot be further built on the vague hope of continuous growth in international trade. As it is true that international inflation is based on single countries and their enterprises, so international employment must start with national economies. In fact, there is a clear example of the possibility of regaining full employment without reliance upon foreign trade expansion, i.e., development during the thirties, especially in Britain and Germany. There also is the paradox that the United States and Canada not only experienced rapid growth and full employment during the Second World War but also raised their real consumption level per head by about 10 to 15 per cent compared to pre-war level (i.e., war for a majority of U.S. and Canadian citizens meant a growth of welfare in traditional terms). This demonstrates that government – not a mystical self-regulating market – is the institution to which to apply for full employment.

In this context one can look more closely at the interrelations

between the 'social market' philosophy and government
economic policy in the postwar period.

Social Market Policies

During the fifties and the early sixties, the bible of German
economists had been Walter Eucken's 'Foundations of
Economic Policy'.[4] As already indicated, Eucken recommended
an economic policy based upon two types of principles: first,
principles which concern economic freedom, guarantee of
private ownership, money control, etc.; second, the so-called
regulating principles comprising anti-monopoly policy,
minimum wages, and state control of natural monopolies. In
general this describes the economic creed of 'market
conformism,' i.e., government policy measures which conform
to the market. This means that each economic intervention by
the state should be confined to modifying the parameters or
market environment data of the firm; no direct intervention
should be allowed. Of course a creed always needs
interpretation. Thus there are no clear lines between policies
which conform to the market and those which do not. But
nevertheless this neo-liberal approach has shaped and still
determines the economic thought of politicians, business-men,
journalists, and academics, most of whom had an income far
above average and whose jobs were secure – until the first real
recession in 1967.

As previously indicated, economic policy during the first
fifteen years after the war did little about competition or control
of the concentration process. Also, economic expansion did not
endanger price stability,[5] because of both the reservoir of
unemployed labour and a comparatively high savings ratio.
For such reasons, it was widely assumed that there was no need
for demand management. Whenever internal demand
slackened, a new demand-pull came from abroad due to the
latent under-valuation of the Deutschmark. Thus the foreign
sector played the role normally attributed to fiscal policy.[6]

Though full employment was reached at the end of the
nineteen-fifties, and despite the effective ending of East–West

German migration with the building of the Berlin Wall, the boom could continue without labour shortage. A stream of foreign migrant labourers began to pour in from 1961. Nevertheless, over full-employment brought some bottlenecks, and from 1960 the computed wage ratio (earned income to national income, with corrections allowed for the structural change from self-employed to wage-earners) curbed its downward trend and started to rise in the opposite direction.[7] From this period the growth rate of GNP also slowed down.[8] In addition, the discrepancies between private capital formation and lagging expenditure on social overhead capital were felt more severely. In 1961 the first modest revaluation had been forced by the permanent surpluses on the current balance of trade. Confidence wanted. For the first time, there was an at least partial questioning of the basis of the Social Market philosophy.

The change has been intimated in cautious policy initiatives through the 1960s. In 1963 a so-called 'Independent Expert Council' had been established, the *Sachverständigenrat zur Begutachtung der gesamtwirtschaftlichen Lage* – and it was generally hoped that this council would elaborate an independent and scientifically-based economic strategy, including moral persuasion, especially against wage demands. Wage demands were increasingly considered inflationary, after the flow of labourers coming from East Germany was cut off at the beginning of the sixties. The council of economic advisers propagated a concept of 'cost-neutral' wage policy, basically opposing unions' aims for income redistribution. Then four years later – 1967 – there was the so-called 'Stability Act'.[9] This act was created in connection with the first really significant economic crisis, starting from the autumn of 1966, which also prompted a change of government. It was the first time that the Social-Democrats (SPD) entered the government via the so-called 'big coalition' with the Christian Democrats. This big coalition pushed through the new Stability Act, and only such a coalition could do it because this act – itself a symptom of the significance of change – could only be established by changing the constitution, which required a two-thirds majority in Parliament and in the Bundestag, as well as in the Federal Council (*Bundesrat*).

Late Keynesianism

The Stability Act brought Keynesian interventionism into the economic philosophy of the German government, and the main points of the act went further – there even was a shade of planning in its approach. But this planning approach was illusory – at least, the main planning characteristics have disappeared again. The first point of the act was an obligation on the government – that means the federal government (*Bund*) and the governments of the states (*Länder*) – to plan their budgets in a five-year period, and especially to plan public investment. Second – there was a prescription for government to reduce debts or to deposit tax money at the *Bundesbank*, i.e., the Central Bank, in times of excess demand. Third – there was provision to speed up investment programmes in times of slack demand and to pay subsidies for investment by local authorities. Fourth, there was the possibility of restricting or postponing public investment if this was initiated by the federal government. Fifth, it became possible to increase the payment of income and corporation taxes, or lower them, for one year, within the margin of plus or minus 10 per cent. Sixth, provision was made to change depreciation rates. Seventh, the federal government authorized that the social security institutions be required during a period to invest a part of their liquid funds in special securities of limited negotiability – that meant a special measure for the open market policy of the central bank, to give it a better chance to manage the money supply by selling or buying state bonds. Further the government was obliged to publish annual projections of the economy, including orientation-data for fiscal and monetary policy.

The last measure approached was a kind of planned incomes policy. A special institution was established called 'concerted action' (*Konzertierte Aktion*), which meant a meeting for mutual information between labour, capital and the state, i.e., unions, employers, government and, of course, the omnipresent central bank. This concerted action was intended to create guidelines for a wage policy accepted by the parties to the discussion, and to establish a kind of centralized bargaining. But in practice this failed, because the unions knew perfectly well that if they agreed to centralized bargaining they would not have any further chance for flexible reactions against inflationary losses of real wages at industry level.

In general, if the idea of a centralized incomes policy through 'concerted action' didn't work as intended, it nevertheless publicized data which was used to influence public opinion in favour of employers (especially through the assumption that wages should be 'neutral' in respect to inflation). So the main points of the Stability Act concern new dimensions to demand management, in particular the possibilities of middle-range planning of public investment for the federal and state governments and the possibility of financing this by the necessary financial measures, including credits which did not need a special authorization by parliament, of up to 5 billion Deutschmarks.

But there were no new instruments for regional and sectoral policy. There also was a further question of what could be done if the permitted demand management scope proved insufficient.

Up to the 1960s government intervention had been confined, as already mentioned, to competition policy and a large dose of social policy of the kind implied in the term 'social market'. In other words, in the hey-day of 'social market' ideology, there had been no intention to plan, or even to coordinate the investment of state-owned companies. Therefore, the recession of 1966, which gave a boost to Keynesian thinking, also caused an ideological crisis for the concept of 'social market economy' which until those days had been essentially anti-Keynesian. The shift to a more Keynesian, or full Keynesian, policy also meant more scope for a new generation of economic ideologists. The great hope they had was that they could prevent each further crisis by aggregate demand management, and at first glance one could get the impression that this formula in the years 1967–8 was successful. The German economy recovered fairly rapidly from recession, and it was believed that this upswing was the result of the new economic philosophy. I don't want to argue about this view: whether it was correct or whether other circumstances (i.e., foreign trade) were the main reason for the revival in 1967–8. It has already been pointed out that there was at the time a very strong export boom – much stronger than the domestic growth of fiscal induced demand.[10]

In any case, confidence in Keynesian policies waned after 1971–2 because of the high inflation rate[11] – high, that is, compared to our experience during the twenty years from 1950 to 1970, however low compared to the international inflation level. Germany had always been on the bottom of the international inflation ladder, but nevertheless, in Germany, the inflation rate is an important political fact which gives the opposition ample chance to campaign against the government. The so-called small coalition (Social Democrats/Liberals) which was formed in 1969 showed after 1970 what power inflation can bring to the opposition benches. Therefore, fiscal policy after 1972–3 was concentrated on an anti-inflationary course. In this economic landscape very conservative political beliefs quickly took root. For instance, some politicians spoke about the re-privatization of the employment risk, which is just another expression for the monetarist 'natural rate' of unemployment. And of course a 'moderate' incomes policy, which meant low wage rates, found much acclamation among big business.

There also was an increased tendency to believe that competition policy would again be the best weapon against inflation. At the beginning of the seventies the fear of inflation brought back conservative arguments, including certain union circles. During this revival of more-or-less anti-Keynesian philosophy, and monetarist pondering upon anti-inflationary measures, the process of concentration of capital went remorselessly on.

Big Business and the State

The concentration of economic power in big business not only changes the traditional market mechanism and the socio-economic structure, but also establishes new relations between the state and the private sector.

The argument on the role of big business has recently taken new analytical directions, which are worth stressing at this point. The concentration of economic power in big business now is so great that it can counterbalance and even manipulate state intervention to its own ends. This power structure of big business *between* the macro and micro levels of the economy has recently been identified – rightly – as a new *meso*-economic structure.[12] Meso-economics in this sense has, of course, been criticized. But such critics of the new approach might well recollect Immanuel Kant's observation that while concepts without empirical perception are empty, empirical perception without a concept is blind. The new power structures of big business need a new conceptual framework of the kind which meso-economics provides.

For instance, traditionally, small-scale capitalist firms have been conceived as an ensemble of separate enterprises, linked by the information mechanism of the market. The direct relations between state and enterprise were negligible. Consequently it was assumed that the political superstructure of the system needed no planned relationship between the state and private enterprise; i.e., no conscious agreement between private capitalism and the capitalist state. In practice, however, the big corporation urged the state to involve itself directly with big business; for instance, there is no bankruptcy of big enterprise today where the state is not called upon to intervene in some form. Wage levels are regulated by the needs of big firms; monopoly control, prices control, monetary measures, and especially exchange rates are managed according to the needs of big corporations. Economic policy gets an overall bias towards the needs of the meso-sector. But this does not necessarily foster economic growth and accumulation, above all because the bias is still undertaken within a capitalist framework. The situation also shows other contradictions. For instance, the need for long-term planning of investment in big firms (large-scale production, high cost of investment items, slower turnover of capital, etc.) requires an equivalent planning of public expenditures. But this would entail a relatively comprehensive planning system of the whole economy, which could not be managed without a broad consensus. In turn, such a major social agreement would need new methods of 'co-determination' and more democracy, and as a corollary would reduce capitalist owner-power. Thus the contradiction. The big

firm needs the planning cake but does not like its democratic
ingredients.

Some figures on concentration in the Federal Republic
should demonstrate the now central importance of big business.
Turnover figures for 1972 show that 103 companies with more
than one billion Deutschmarks turnover undertook 43 per cent
of the total investment in manufacturing, trade, and transport
combined. The 30 biggest companies had a share of 35 per cent
of total investment. The concentration of turnover figures
shows an even more impressive figure. In 1964, the top
hundred companies in manufacturing represented 41 per
cent of the total turnover; by 1974 their share had risen to
56 per cent.[13]

Obviously this concentration of economic power has
outdated the division of economic theory in micro- and macro-
economics. A meso-economic sector with its own economic and
political qualities has emerged. According to the traditional
approach, micro-economics studies the behaviour of numerous
individual decision units, whereas macro-economics deals with
economic aggregates – consumption, investment, and so on.
Conventional economic policy reflects this duality – micro-
competition policy is supposed to secure or to re-establish the
market mechansim, and macro-stabilization policy is supposed
to assure a global management of demand aggregates.
According to the conventional wisdom, global demand-
orientated macro-policies are disaggregated by the market
mechanism at the micro level into production and investment
decisions by the numerous firms. However, this doctrine
overlooks the autonomy of the new meso-economic sector,
which already controls more than 50 per cent of private
production and investment.

The Case for Planning

It is this new meso-economic power which makes it imperative
to transform the previous indirect combination of competition
policy and demand management of the Keynesian type and to
introduce a structural policy directly influencing private

investment. But this needs a new information system which can be provided only by economic planning.

Around 1972 intensive discussion started in Germany about the need to change from a competition based and demand-management-orientated economic policy to a policy of more direct intervention in private investment. This means plan-orientated intervention and instruments for an implementation of the plan, especially to influence the volume and structure of private investment.[14] There should be a combination of the following factors.

First, there has to be a socio-economic plan ranging to at least a five years' horizon. This plan should demonstrate a structural strategy for the economy.

Second, there is the key question of implementation.[15] The new influence upon private investment decisions should be based upon new information, and exercised through so-called indirect measures such as subsidies and taxes, plus – probably the most crucial point in the discussion – the power of temporary investment veto. That means that the state should be able to forbid certain private investment and provoke a shift into another direction. To get the necessary information basis, we need a registration of projected private investment. Norbert Wieczorek's contribution elaborates this point more completely, but I just want to mention one important aspect – namely, the registration of projected private investment. That means to collect, collate, and use information which is already available at a decentralized level; it needs only new legislation to obtain existing information. This is a point that is stressed both by the unions and by the Social Democratic party.[16] Maybe this does not seem a major advance, but it shows that there are new perspectives on the handling of private investment which now go beyond the social market or Keynesian philosophies.[17]

A third point concerns the nature of the new strategy for investment control. The premise is that decisions should remain de-centralized in principle. This is a case stressed by Giorgio Ruffolo and other contributors to this study, yet opposed by some sections of the Left. On the other hand, all the important private investment plans should be registered and submitted to a form of strategic control. This could be managed by investment licences. These licences should be given according to the priorities of the socio-economic plan, supplemented by short-run stabilization considerations and other accepted norms – for instance, protection of the environment.

These points should indicate that the concept of investment planning and its implementation differ significantly from that in the centrally planned economies, in flexibility, and by the fact that there is not – at least not in the first phase – any kind of socialization of the means of production or direct price policy. Of course, when viewed from abroad, these proposals may seem to be very timid. But critics from elsewhere have to take account of the special situation in West Germany. The fact that the economy enjoyed a very steady period of growth without incisive state intervention for about 15 years is still very much remembered and leads to substantial public scepticism about planning. Besides, Germany still has a very strong anti-communist and anti-plan ideology. The confrontation with East Germany always fosters anti-planning arguments. It is against this political and ideological background that the discussion about investment control and planning has to be seen and understood.

6

Perspectives for Planning

Norbert Wieczorek

'Plan,' in the Federal Republic of West Germany, is very much a four-letter word. To understand why, one has to look both at geography and history. The nearby experience of planning in the DDR, over the border, is enough in itself to make the concept of democratic planning unimaginable to many Germans. The history of planning in the Third Reich only confirms the prejudice against planning in general. Besides which, the economy of the Federal Republic has experienced a so-called miracle of growth and export capacity which for years has made it a model for other countries. Many Germans hold to the miracle and espouse its myth despite the current crisis in the economy and the evident need for a fundamental rethinking of economic policy.

Socialization versus Social Market

To gain perspectives on the possibility of new forms of democratic planning in Germany, one has to go back in some detail, at least to the immediate postwar period. Ironically, at that stage, there was a relatively broad, if temporary, consensus on the need for socialization, not only in the Social Democratic Party but also in the Christian Democrats. The latter party initially accepted the case for public ownership of basic industry and the banks, because at that time, there was a clearer grasp of the extent to which Nazi intervention in the economy had been based on a close association between private big business and the state. But what happened was a metamorphosis of this initial commitment into something superficially similar and essentially different.

The change was from socialization to the 'social market' philosophy. This concept, raised by the Christian Democrats into a prevailing ideology, was subtle and highly intelligent. In fact it masked the market forces which re-established big business in a dominant position in the German economy. But by calling the market 'social' rather than 'private' or even 'free,' the impression was generated of a market mechanism both serving the general interest and in which the public in general could play an equal part. The concept of a democratic economy, disguised the plutocracy and inequality of the system. In principle, everyone was free to buy what he wanted or did not want, disguising the fact that some consumers and some firms were significantly more equal than others in their relative market power.

Besides, the working of the market in the postwar period did fulfil the basic needs of the West German people. They had enough food, which was itself important granted that many of them had been starving before. They were clothed, and they were sheltered. By the mid 1950s, in comparison either with the immediate postwar period or the 1930s, they had achieved what appeared to be relative luxury. Inequality in the distribution of income, wealth, or power seemed unimportant to most people because they had more than before. Added to the experience of the so-called Democratic Republic nearby, where living standards were lower, the concept of socialist planning seemed either sinister or bizarre. The Stalinism of the régime in the DDR, and the apparent readiness of its leaders to consider Moscow the wisest city in the world, did not recommend itself – understandably enough – in West Germany.

Workers' Participation Reviewed

In addition, some of the reforms established in the postwar period appeared to give working people a significant say in the control and running of enterprise. For instance, in the coal and steel industries the system of qualified *Mitbestimmung* gave workers' representatives 49 per cent of the voting power on the supervisory boards of companies. Shareholders also had 49 per cent of voting power, with the balance held by a so-called neutral individual. In addition to such qualified *Mitbestimmung*, established in 1952, workers were given some other rights to control working conditions in companies through what was known as the *Betriebsverfassungsgesetz*. Some later reforms extended these rights to a say in hiring and firing, and also to certain information on the companies concerned. While this fell short of workers' control, it nevertheless has given workers, especially in iron and steel, a feeling of what is going on in a company. If their trade unions are enterprising, they can use such legislation to considerable effect.

Nevertheless, in general, little happened after 1952 to extend the rights of workers over enterprise or the economy. In fact, especially following real United States commitment through Marshall Aid, there was a regression against the philosophy of socialist intervention and social control of the economy. The success of reconstruction, with American support, established a hegemony of the Erhard ideology, based on the ideas of Walter Eucken, which has been analysed in the previous chapter by Karl Georg Zinn. The KPD or Communist Party was declared unconstitutional, and had to go underground. In the Social Democratic Party a struggle ensued between people who more or less accepted the social market philosophy and others who remained committed to earlier socialist ideas. This struggle was won, without doubt, by the advocates of the social market philosophy.

The Godesberg Programme

This can be seen in the Godesberg Programme of the SPD, which was adopted in 1959.[1] The Programme still contains reference to earlier socialist ideas. For instance, it admits that socialization through public ownership and investment control may be necessary to countervail private economic power – but only where other policies including competition policy have been shown not to work. There is no doubt that the Programme in general endorsed the general line of the social market philosophy, and no one who is familiar with the main elements of the Godesberg Programme can be surprised at the liberal market policies pursued subsequently by Social Democratic ministers. When principles of Keynesian demand management were applied in government by Mr. Schiller as Economics Minister, they were wedded to the assumption of a competitive market process on the supply side of industry and services. The progress was not beyond neoclassical economics of the market, but towards a Keynesian neoclassical synthesis.

Superficially, the rapid recovery of the economy from the first major postwar recession, in 1966–7, maintained the impression that nothing was fundamentally amiss with the social market. But by 1969 there had been a series of strikes provoked substantially by the form of Keynesian policies which Schiller had introduced. In other words, his demand management had been good for profits, but less good for wages. This was combined with increased student unrest and a radicalization of student politics. The demand for major reforms in the nature of the economic and social system, rather than mere management of the social market, was placed dramatically on the political agenda. Moreover, the reforms demanded extended also to foreign policy, in the shape of what was to become known as the *Ostpolitik* and a new readiness to admit realities in the international sphere.

In practice this amounted to a turning-point in both opinion and politics. There was a connection, of course, with the new demands and the new thinking which occurred in France following May 1968, with its indirect impact on mainstream politics and opinion in France. The ultra-Left pursued its own politics in its own ways, which are well enough known, if not notorious. But the main arena for debate on new options for the economy and society in Germany took place within the Social Democratic Party. I stress the SPD as a party rather than the more familiar term of 'labour movement,' because German trade unions since the war have followed a practice of much greater nominal neutrality in politics than their British counterparts, or some unions in France and Italy. There are, of course, close enough links with the SPD and political commitment at higher levels of the trade unions. But the formal neutrality remains, reflecting a reality in which some 40 per cent of trade union members in fact vote for the Christian Democratic Party.

Towards a Radical Programme

The new debate and pressure for change in the SPD was expressed in the 1969 Party Congress, which endorsed the formulation of a Long-Term Programme. It is important to admit that there was a very long delay between the decision to undertake such a programme and its publication – in 1975.[2] One reason for this was the general hold of the social market philosophy among leading personalities in the party, and especially in the government. Put simply, many of the older guard in the party did not see the need for a major rethinking of economic policy and political strategy. It was no coincidence that the chairman of the party commission for formulation of the long-term programme was the then Minister of Finance and now Chancellor, Helmut Schmidt.

The case for a new long-term strategy was promoted at regional party level, and strongly advocated by the JuSos, or Young Socialists, within the SPD. To be a Young Socialist in Germany does not mean late adolescence or even exceptional youth. It means any party member up to the age of thirty-five. As a result this included a very wide range of SPD membership – up to a third of the total – and a powerful pressure group within the party and the movement. Some of the principal economic recommendations, which later were established in the Long-Term Programme of the party, were proposals for new investment coordination and structural policy in the economy. They were seen, with reason, as new proposals for economic and social planning.

The new case argued that the German economy was faced with major structural change which could not be 'adjusted' through a combination of competition policy and demand management. These were the kinds of changes analysed in the previous chapter by Karl Georg Zinn, including a trend to private consumer saturation, investment slump, and structural unemployment. We argued that the economic crisis emerging in the late 1960s necessitated major changes in both production and consumption – a change from private to public spending, on the one hand, and from private to public control of investment, on the other.

We saw investment very much as the key to change. After all, investment decisions concern what will be produced, where it will be produced, for what market, and to whose benefit. It implies production for a specific structure of consumption and demand. The question of whose benefit, of course, is crucial. It entails the question of production on private criteria or on social criteria. Also, a new framework for reasoning and bargaining on investment makes possible a widened role for working people and trade unions in the use of resources in society. It means planning, but should not mean the bureaucratic planning, from the centre, of resource use in society. German trade unions are strong, and rightly defend the gains which they have already achieved, however limited, within some companies (especially the public sector firms). They are not so starry-eyed, or misled, as to accept any targets or objectives decided at a higher level and handed down from above.

Put differently, investment control, as an issue and a policy within the SPD, meant raising not only new questions on the structure and use of resources in society, but also an extended control for working people over the decision on how resources should be used. It opened the prospect of planning within an extended framework of industrial democracy.

There are clear enough parallels here with the new terms of debate on planning on the Left in other Western European countries. The same is true of the analysis of changes in economic structure, and especially big business domination, with its potential for new instruments to secure democratic control of resource allocation. Karl Georg Zinn has already shown the major concentration of economic power in the economy of the Federal Republic, and related it to analysis of meso-economic structures between the micro level of smaller firms' market mythology and the macro level of overall economic performance. The new proposals for investment coordination, as in Labour's Programmes in Britain in the seventies, were focused on leading firms.

The focus on big business and the need to ensure mechanisms for its social control through planning make sense of the case for as much centralization as is necessary, with as much decentralization as is possible. Superficially, this compares with the terminology of the Godesberg Programme, which had argued that there should be as much planning as is necessary and as much market as possible. But with the debate on the new Long-Term Programme, the whole term of reference had been changed. For instance, instead of waiting for evidence that competition policy had been tried and failed before public intervention in individual firms or industries, the new proposals demand advance revelation of information from leading firms, to the government, on the broad range of their investment programmes. Put differently, the new programme demands the revelation of corporate planning to the government to put it in a position to contribute to the overall planning of the economy.

Immediately, one should introduce a practical *caveat*. One is the role played by the Constitution of the Federal Republic in the whole debate on ownership of the means of production. Our written constitution embodies certain 'basic rights'. One of there is the right of control by individuals over the means of production, which in practice is widely taken to mean the right to private enterprise. Article 15 of the Constitution specifies that socialization of the means of production can be undertaken where it is necessary for the economic welfare and development of the Federal Republic. But one also has to be in a position to show that private enterprise has been acting knowingly against the accepted framework of economic policy. In other words, the questions of public ownership and planning almost immediately raise a constitutional tangle of major dimensions

In itself, of course, this need not prove a permanent obstacle to their adoption in government. If, for instance, a party won a general election on the grounds of extended socialization and planning, it is unlikely that the constitutional barrier would prove definitive. Either a new 'finding' by the constitutional court or a formal revision of the constitution would be on the agenda. But the provisions at present play into the hands of conservative forces, both outside and inside the SPD. They reinforce both inertia and negative opposition to change.

One area where this could be important is the revelation of information on corporate planning to the government. We know already, from experience in Britain, where the CBI launched a major campaign against the revelation of such information for Planning Agreements, that private enterprise and its pressure groups would be likely to claim breach of confidentiality and the loss of commercial advantage. Similarly, there is likely to be considerable opposition to the principle of licences for investment, which form an important part our investment-coordination proposals in the big league sector. There is little doubt that compromise pressure, rather than licences, would be exerted for selective incentives as a mechanism for inducing investment change rather than ensuring strategic control. But as the British experience has already shown, there are strong grounds for doubting the effectiveness of incentives as an exclusive mechanism for influencing investment.

In other words, if there is to be real advance towards new forms of planning and social control in the Federal Republic, it will not be without political advocacy and political struggle. The objective of the new measures is to change what occurs in the economy. This itself will not occur unless the trade unions themselves become involved as advocates of planning, and as pressure groups for the translation of what now is in the Long-Term Programme of the SPD into action in government.

At present there is evidence of a new radicalization among some unions and union leadership. One sign is the pressure to move from a 49 per cent to 50 per cent union vote on the supervisory boards of companies. This pressure is important in itself. But it also is important to move beyond the internal democracy of the enterprise to the role that leading enterprise plays in the economy at large. And this raises the question of the role trade unions should play in the setting of new and different targets for big business in the system.

That is why we have proposed that the Economic and Social Council (*Wirtschafts-und-Sozialrat*) should be be constructed on a tri-partite basis, meaning involvement of government, trade unions, and companies – bearing in mind that, as indicated above, the supervisory boards of companies should themselves involve 50 per cent trade union voting and control power. We have argued that the Council should formulate the overall targets or plan for the economy, with its legal endorsement, subject to debate and ratification in the *Bundestag* or parliament.

This new proposal was fought very hard within the SPD and debated widely within the public at large. This emerged very clearly from the 1973 conference of the SPD at Hanover. It was not so much that the conference decisively endorsed the proposals, as that it rejected the draft of the Long-Term Programme as devised by Helmut Schmidt. In itself, this was a major political advance. The specific proposals for investment coordination and structural policy, which hitherto had been endorsed only on a regional party basis, advanced on to the platform of primary debate within the SPD itself at a national level. It translated the terms of the debate from relatively esoteric discussion among *cognoscenti* to familiar terms of reference on economic policy in national debate. It also paved the way for adoption of the key elements in the new proposals in the Long-Term Programme as accepted by the SPD congress at Mannheim in 1975.

The Mannheim Programme

The Mannheim Programme self-consciously cross-refers to the Godesberg Programme, in terms of the role of the market, of public enterprise, and investment control. As with the Godesberg Programme itself there is a clear effort to get the best of both worlds. On the other hand, there also clearly is commitment to a general critique of contemporary capitalism and to a specific strategy for change which represents a major advance within the SPD. There still is endorsement of instruments such as competition policy and an on-going role for the market. But the context has changed. Instead of a move towards conservative or Christian Democratic policies of the social market variety, there is a move towards more direct measures for the attainment of social criteria and fulfilment of social values through intervention. As opposed to the

Godesberg adaptation to the *Wirtschaftswunder*, and its implicit assumption that the social market economy works, there is an essential admission that German capitalism is in crisis, and that there is a need for socialist planning.

In other words, while the Godesberg Programme represented a compromise with capitalism and a decline of socialist thinking in the SPD, the Mannheim Long-Term Programme represents a challenge to capitalist thinking and a reassertion of the case for socialist planning.

Of course, while the Mannheim congress endorsed a Long-Term Programme, the government controls the short to medium-term policies without which there will be no long-term change. In this sense there is a clear question of the relations between political power and state power in the SPD, parallel to that in the Labour movement in other countries such as Britain in the seventies.

The Role of the Unions

The chance of translating the Programme into reality, as elsewhere abroad, very much depend on the role of the trade unions and their relations with the government. I have already stressed that the formal links between the SPD and the German trade unions are somewhat different from a country such as Britain. The German TUC – DGB – is more careful to maintain a nominal neutrality from particular parties. On the other hand, in practice, the struggle and debate within the SPD which resulted in the shaping and adoption of the Long-Term Programme clearly have not gone unnoticed within the trade unions. In fact, a conference of the DGB in 1975 discussed the policy of investment coordination or *Investitionslenking*, as well as the question of the voting share of workers on supervisory boards and the right to control new aspects of working conditions within companies (*Mitbestimmung* and *Betriebsverfassungsgesetz*).

There is no doubt that the underlying crisis of the economy plays a key role in the interest of the unions in more radical economic policies. Karl Georg Zinn has already drawn attention to the fact that registered unemployment in the Federal Republic would be much higher if it had not been for the repatriation of some two-thirds of a million 'guest-workers'. German unions clearly are well aware that there is a structural crisis of investment and employment which is not going to be resolved by older style policies of indirect intervention. Therefore they have become much more interested in questions of structural and regional policy as debated and formulated within the SPD, which implies the need for targets and planning. Indeed, by the end of 1976 the head of the DGB, Mr. Vetter, made plain in a series of public statements that if social market policies were going to mean permanent structural unemployment of around a million, the government had better rethink its commitment to the social market philosophy.[3]

Vetter's public criticism of the government was no accident. It reflected increasing conviction among trade unionists that the alternative economic strategy of the SPD, embodied in the Long-Term Programme, was both credible and necessary. It also is no secret that various working parties within the trade union movement have been considering the feasibility of the radical alternatives to the social market.

This structured consideration of new perspectives for social and economic policy also is paralleled within the SPD itself. For instance, the main economic commission of the party used to be a huge talking shop to which anyone came who had something to say about economics. It was a sounding board for opinion – praiseworthy enough in itself, but at the cost of an effective committee of the party for the scrutiny and countervailance of government economic policy. In 1976 this body was transformed into a small working group, with prospects of a real capacity for party monitoring of government economic policy, and for formulation of on-going policies in relation to the structural problems of the economy.

Planning for Change

However, there also is another prospect, which should not be discounted. This is the probability that German big business in fact will shift its ideological ground and move away from the social market philosophy to demands for planning by its values and in its interests. It is in such a context that the formulation of the SPD's Long-Term Programme, and its adoption at the 1975 Mannheim congress, is of major importance. The Programme gives a perspective on planning for social and structural change in the economy, with specific targets set via the democratic process, rather than private criteria for the restructuring of capital on its own terms. It provides a framework for criticism and countervailance of drift towards capitalist planning.

The Long-Term Programme also is important, since with its emphasis on structural change it gives a key term of reference to challenge the drift towards permanently high levels of unemployment. This is important in terms of the political credibility of the SPD during the present period of economic crisis in the Federal Republic. The association between high unemployment and reaction from the Right was well enough established between the wars. Even in the brief recession of 1966–7 the vote for the neo-facist NPD rose to over five per cent, and up to 10 per cent in some state or *Land* elections. The increase in civil and political tensions in 1977, with the problems of terrorism, has created a climate in which it is crucial that democratic planning for social and economic justice is seen to be credible and feasible by a wide section of the electorate.

None of this will be easy. Not least, it is important that there should be a framework and climate for intervention at the international level. The parallelism between the problems and prospects for planning in West Germany and other Western European countries is greater than many outside Germany imagine. The similarity between the strategy of the Long-Term Programme as adopted at Mannheim and the programmes of socialist and social democratic parties in other countries is important. There are major problems, especially on the nature and status of joint action through EEC institutions. Nevertheless, there is scope for joint action on the European Left to counter the trend towards corporatism and capitalist planning – not least through increased awareness of the convergence of policies for democratic socialist planning which this book illustrates.

PART IV

British Malpractice

7

Britain's Planning Problems
Thomas Balogh

The problem of planning in Britain has undergone very startling changes. It could well be illustrated by the changing fashion in young ladies' dress over recent years: it has had its 'mini' and 'maxi' periods. I shall try to analyse these in a historical context, and to relate them to the current issues of planning in Britain.

There was a 'maxi' planning period immediately after the war. This was a period in which wartime controls of the economy were carried over into postwar shortages and austerity. Naturally enough, the association of austerity with planning was not highly persuasive. But, in addition, the postwar civil service was denuded of committed planners as its wartime reinforcements returned to civilian employment. Bereft of their commitment and skills, the lack of training and lack of commitment to planning in the civil service were asserted in the form of a violent reaction against planning. It was in this climate that the then President of the Board of Trade Mr. Harold (now Sir Harold) Wilson committed a bonfire of controls.

Clearly, such de-control undermined the basis for effective planning. Indeed, after the 1947 fuel crisis – during an exceptionally hard winter – and after the 1949 sterling crisis, which resulted in an excessive devaluation of sterling, planning became a pejorative word. Pro-planners were accused of holding that Whitehall knew best, and it was claimed in exaggerated fashion that systematic planning would lead to serfdom.[1] This phase was followed by a vast unplanned increase in rearmament, vehemently supported by Mr. Hugh Gaitskell. Of all people, he was primarily responsible for our present troubles. Rearmament killed stone dead the successful export-based expansion which between 1945 and 1949 reconquered our markets lost during the war. Ever since, we have aspired to start again but never succeeded. The insufficient capacity of steel, engineering, and the related armaments industry was overburdened. We were caught in the toils of insufficient investment, leading to premature shortages sucking in imports, and ending all possibility of recreating an export-led expansion. The premature decontrol of imports was an additional curse on our prosperity. I think that on the whole one might say that this is a lesson which has yet to be learned, because we are again in a situation in which a replay of this tragedy is possible.

Then, of course, came the great period of relief. The rearmament, of course, was a result of the Korean War's coming after the Berlin Blockade and the conquest of Czechoslovakia by the Soviets in 1948. Again, there are some contemporary resemblances. The Korean War, like the 1972–3 boom ending in the oil embargo, turned the terms of trade violently against us. The Treasury's planning capacity – or lack of it – was amply demonstrated by the fact that they succeeded in abolishing certain free dental services and spectacles, saving 36 million pounds a year, only to be overwhelmed by an increase in imports of 600 millions, as a result of the need to restock food and raw materials. Almost immediately after the election of 1951, which dismissed the Labour Government, there was an equally violent turn of the terms of trade in our favour. This handed to the victorious Conservative Government a present of something like 10 per cent of the national income, perhaps even more.

The Wasted Years

This turn in the terms of trade gave an uncovenanted bonus to Britain. At the same time rearmament was severely cut back by the Churchill government. The resources made available were thereby further vastly increased. They ought to have been ploughed back into productive investment so as to strengthen the economy and enable it to stand up to its rivals. At that point Britain could still have taken a lead in planning. It did not. The bonus was frittered away through decontrol and liberalization, through an enormous increase in home consumption and more especially consumption of durable goods. The Butler period of decontrol between 1951 and 1955–6 was one of the most successful, so to speak, *consumer-led* booms in the postwar history of Western Europe. There was a sort of elation at the ease with which we dispensed with 'artificial' interference with the market mechanism, a kind of miracle. The Germans had their 'miracle,' the French theirs and we had our 'miracle.' Only our 'miracle' did not strengthen the country. It weakened it.

The next thing which happened, of course, was that you can't consume twice what you have got, and as a result of this liberalization we ran into difficulties with our exports, first in 1955. By 1957 the repetitive character of our malaise became quite clear. The 'go' was followed by a 'stop'. There was the famous row in Cabinet about cutbacks in expenditure leading to the 'little local difficulty,' as Mr. Macmillan called it, when Mr. Thorneycroft, egged on by Mr. Enoch Powell, resigned over the rejection of their proposal to cut back the budget by a hundred million pounds. How long ago those days when a hundred million led to resignations. . . . But however small the sum, the pattern emerges: despite the turning terms of trade that caused the crisis of 1951, a balance of payments problem arose,[2] and this was repeated in 1961, and again in 1964. In between 1957 and 1961 there was an election, and democratic countries in election years usually have booms. We followed the pattern and we paid for it afterwards. The Conservative government panicked, seven Ministers were sacked (about a quarter of the whole Cabinet), including Selwyn Lloyd, the Chancellor.

The National Economic Development Council

Now Selwyn Lloyd left a legacy which was to cause him some difficulty. This legacy was the National Economic Development Council (NEDC). For the first time the British government acknowledged that an institutional arrangement was needed between Ministers, the Civil Service, and the two sides of industry. It was at last and none too early accepted that the Civil

Service was not trained for planning. However adequate they may have been for a night-watchman state (and even this is doubtful) they were not adapted to the requirements of a modern industrial state. The NEDC therefore was strengthened by an economic staff.

The old situation in which the economists were kept, as the saying goes, on tap but not on top, altered. I have to admit that this change, an important change, was not sufficient to change our fate, because when the economists were moved from tap to top the economic situation did not improve. A step towards planning was taken. A separate planning agency was established, with professional economists manning it. The action and counter-action of these two focal points – the Civil Service, which wanted to try to keep out of trouble, and the National Economic Development Council, which wanted to plan – was interesting. The two tendencies and the two professional interests obviously clashed.

The National Economic Development Council wanted to prove how much one could achieve, whereas the Treasury economists (the economic section of the Treasury inherited from the Cabinet Office where they had been established during the War, but shrunk in importance within the Civil Service) were as usual cautious. While in the Cabinet Office, the economic section had access to a number of Ministers. As a special section of the Treasury, they didn't even have direct access to the Chancellor of the Exchequer, except for the head, who was from time to time, but not very often, consulted. Unfortunately it will take another fifteen years to get access to the papers – until then one cannot really know what exactly happened, but some little light has been thrown like a sort of laser beam on certain special points in the evidence submitted to the so-called Bank Rate Leak Tribunal. And one has the impression, but it *is* only an impression, that the Chancellor of the Exchequer did *not* consult the head of the economic section in most of his decisions in this period. So whatever they had advocated does not seem to have penetrated – and there were some extremely interesting and very able economists in the economic section. For instance Jack Downie – who wrote by far the best book on oil and oligopolistic price-fixing.[3]

There was no doubt that there had been a clash between the NEDC and the Treasury. The first plan was produced by NEDC in 1962–3. This projected a $4\frac{1}{2}$ per cent increase in the national income and made a very plausible-looking plan of how it should be distributed, and how it should be used. As an exercise in indicative planning, it wasn't too bad. It was not so much a plan as a target which, had it worked, would have been useful. However, it was an unfortunate moment for this sort of an exercise. After the 1959 election boom Britain had run into very severe balance of payments problems and the 'stop-go' cycle yet again returned to 'stop', with Britain suffering a relatively high rate of unemployment for the first time since the War, though it was not anything as serious as it was to become.

The most ominous aspect about these 'stop-go' cycles was that at each recovery one recovered less, and at each slump one lost more employment than before, while the deficits in the balance of payments continued to increase. And underlying this sign of *malaise* there was a continuous shrinkage of employment in manufacturing. It is doubtful that this trend can be explained on Keynesian lines on the basis of demand deficiency. It is more likely that it is due to the basic unsoundness of the economy, not merely pre-Keynesian but pre-capitalist, paralleling other half-developed countries rather than the kind which recently plagued the US or Germany.

At this point once more, when the NEDC prepared its plan, an election approached. Mr. Maudling, the new Chancellor, consequently tried to get the unemployment figure down. It was impossible to generate an export-based boom except by devaluation followed up by an agreement with the trade unions to moderate their wage claims. This was ruled out, although, given the level of unemployment, it just might have worked. Unfortunately the policy of the previous Chancellor pre-empted such an agreement. Once more a domestic, consumption-orientated expansion was stimulated with baneful consequences to the balance of payments. It had little of the inspiration of the NEDC plan.

The great difference between this sort of planning and French planning is that the French plan was fashioned for a moderately but steadily expanding economy, especially between 1958 and

1968. Therefore the plan-makers had to restrict investment rather than encourage it. Now restriction is easy, especially if one controls the tuning system; encouragement in an unfavourable atmosphere with entrepreneurs anticipating renewed restrictions is very difficult. Keynes once said, 'You can pull with a string, but you can't push with it.' The would-be British planners were given an all but impossible task: to give an internal impulse for expansion through increased investment, and to prevent it from causing a balance of payments crisis – devaluation and protection being ruled out.

But an increase of productive investment was all but impossible in a situation where excess capacity was considerable. The dilemma of current economic politics was that if the government wanted to keep a fixed parity for sterling, it would need to deflate as the election approached. Naturally, it was bewildered by so unpleasant and politically impossible a scenario. Short-run success in cutting unemployment was needed. Maudling, therefore, could not be choosy. He piled on the stimuli for attaining expansion. Once more durable consumer goods had to carry the load, and the restrictions on hire purchase were lifted. The fiscal push was given, not to investment, but to consumption. Unfortunately – just like rearmament – consumption is an extremely dangerous weapon with which to regulate the economy. It will not result in a self-sustaining, strengthening of the economy in face of our industrial rivals. With a relatively weak industrial sector and with all governments, Labour and Conservative, bent on liberalization, the balance of trade duly deteriorated. The first 'plan' of NEDC was aborted.

The Rise and Demise of the National Plan

When the Labour government took over in 1964 a thorough reorganization of the government machine dealing with economics was undertaken. Mr. Wilson had asked me to prepare a paper on the Civil Service on being elected to the Leadership of the Opposition.

I published the result in a Fabian pamphlet, 'Planning for

Progress', and a Fabian working party (of which Professor Neild and I were members) endorsed these conclusions. These were that planning had to be organized inside the government machine. The proposed planning organization (the Department for Economic Affairs) had to be separate from the Treasury because the Treasury had departmental interests (e.g. the maintenance of support from the City, liberalization of capital movements and – at the point of time – the maintenance of the $2.40 parity of the pound)[4] which were not necessarily identical with those of a Labour Government pledged to full employment and intensified investment.

Relative to the claim that planning was a last-minute commitment by Labour before the 1964 election, it may be of interest to quote from *The Four Year Plan* on which Mr. Wilson and I collaborated (*New Statesman*, 24 March 1961). He wrote,

> Economic planning must then be directed first to increasing investment, and to increasing it purposively. The priorities must be the industries which strengthen our industrial base and provide the means to further production, particularly of the goods we can best hope to sell in the markets of the world. The result of this will be threefold. The realization of the plan demands a dramatic and selective increase in investment in the first year. A National Investment Board should be set up, to work out for each major industry, public and private, the rate of expansion needed. The Four Year Plan should provide the publicly-owned industries with a clear investment programme covering the whole period of the plan. It would, of course, be related industry by industry to the investment and export programmes, but once it is settled the industries concerned should have every assurance that they could proceed, unhampered by Government policy changes, for at least four years ahead.

The NEDC from 1964 went into a sort of hibernation. Planning was transferred to the government machine and the newly created Department of Economic Affairs (DEA) was charged with the elaboration of a longer-term plan. One of the results was that very many more professional economists were hired than ever before, and professional economists were put into strategic positions in the important economic departments, as they were speaking the same language, they were able to coordinate policy advice. This was not the case after 1974. So much for George Brown's somewhat fanciful account of the creation of DEA in a taxi ride.[5]

However, there were two grave difficulties militating against the success of this plan. It was a target plan, and as a target plan it could and would have done some good, if it had been supported by a devaluation as soon as the Maudling inflation was under control and a compact was secured with the trade unions. Moreover, DEA unfortunately was not at first put under the Prime Minister with a junior Minister in charge. Thus a struggle ensued between the Treasury and the DEA, which was exacerbated by the personal rivalry of the two Cabinet Ministers concerned. There was a fleeting moment when Peter Shore was put in charge of DEA under the direct supervision of the Prime Minister. At that point this could have represented an effective planning machinery. Unfortunately, this experiment perished prematurely, before it had a chance of showing results. The Treasury dominance reasserted itself with grave consequences to national fortunes.

This, however, is to anticipate. As it was, the balance of payments deteriorated, foreign hot money began to flee from London, and the basic primitive instinct of governments faced with deteriorating balance of payments asserted itself – i.e., monetary and fiscal restriction. This represented a deadly threat to the National Plan, as it was impossible to combine a restrictive policy with an expansionist policy, on which the plan was based. When we at last devalued in 1967 it was too late to resuscitate the plan, especially as, after the wage freeze, inflationary forces could be dealt with only by restrictive policies: incomes policy was given up. This was the basic reason why the plan failed. We then had a very heavy surplus by 1970, which was not used for a forward policy. The Jenkins budget, unemployment and a failed attack on industrial relations, all policies opposed by progressive economists, led to the fall of the government.

In one sense, the problem with the National Plan was that it came at the wrong moment. There was no economist in the 1964–70 government who by March 1966 didn't want to devalue. Now I had been against devaluation in previous debates, but at that point it was evident that we could not get the plan off the ground without it. At the time, we had a sufficient amount of unemployment in order to make the devaluation, like the second French devaluation, stick. The French provide an extraordinarily good example of how and when to devalue, and also how not to devalue. They devalued in 1957, and it was no good at all – indeed it accelerated inflation; but in 1958 they devalued and that did solve their problem and gave them a long-run expansion.

Also, our difficulties arose because we wanted to grow at $4\frac{1}{2}$ per cent, but at the same time there was no sort of internal cohesion between general economic policy and the underlying planning policy. The fact that there were difficulties between the Treasury and the DEA of a more personal nature did not help at all. Generally speaking, informed public opinion (and political action) fluctuated. When it was converted to planning, we were in a situation in which planning was impossible because the 'stop' caused by the deflationary measures of July 1966 had undermined the expansionary climate crucial to effective planning. Unfortunately, one could generalize this and say that when you *could* plan, you don't, and when you *do* plan, you can't.

Monetarism and Incomes Policy

With the failure in planning, and the fall of the Labour government in 1970, Britain was landed into the U-turns of the Heath government, with its Mark I and Mark II phases. The first phase might well be called 'mini-skirt monetarism' by the criteria of my earlier 'mini' and 'maxi' distinctions. This was a conscious turn-round from the attempt to intervene directly on either investment or incomes. With the ensuing sharp rise in unemployment, there was the further turn-round to the Mark II phase, which should properly be called the Heath-Armstrong phase according to at least the press reports of the time, which

attributed the main influence to Sir William (now Lord)
Armstrong, then Head of the Civil Service.

The trouble with the Heath Mark II policy was that it could
not work, because by that time the trade unions had been too far
exacerbated by the Industrial Relations Act and the
aggressiveness of Heath Mark I. Heath's Mark II policy was
quite a sensible one – but, of course, in order to make it
workable the government would have to have the closest cooperation with the trade unions, because planning against or
even without the trade unions cannot work. The aim of planning
is to accelerate economic growth. In order to accelerate
economic growth there has to be fullish employment, for in an
individualist economy investment depends on high demand.
Fullish employment, however, induces a revolutionary break
between the division of national economic power and the
distribution of national income. And this break between these
two leads to friction at the interface. And where is the interface?
It is at the determination of the money wage level. A plan
intended to accelerate economic progress must secure a
reduction of the friction at the interface between the trade
unions, employers, and the government.

This obviously could not be done by the Heath government.
Thus it failed to achieve a sensible policy of phasing a planned
expansion in investment into the economy. Inflation and
unemployment both violently increased, and the miner's strike
finished Heath off. What followed immediately after his fall,
under the Labour government, was influenced by these
traumatic experiences. The unions set their faces against any
imposed policy at all. The 1970 conference of the Labour Party
reflected this. When I pleaded for a comprehensive incomes,
taxation, and social policy embodied in a plan, I was attacked in
the sharpest terms by Mr. Jack Jones, who is a rather recent
convert for incomes policy. Let us leave bygones be bygones.
Then Mr. Jack Jones and Michael Foot and Harold Wilson
accomplished a miraculous turn-around in the attitudes of
trade unions. It may be possible as the next goal to have a
planned incomes policy, a planned investment policy and
perhaps, as a result of that, a combination of high employment,
stability, and the end of balance of payments difficulties.

International Implications

We are not there yet, however. No country has been able to reconstruct its identity (and nothing less is needed in Britain) from a position of weakness without protective measures. It was our misfortune that unlike Japan, Germany, and France we gave up direct controls in an orgy of liberalization, culminating in the entry – without due safeguarding – into the EEC.

EEC entry does not mean that the intellectual case for planning is changed, but of course the weaponry of economic policy has been very much affected. Besides, those of use who did not terribly like the idea of the Common Market felt this way partly because it was one thing to join a club when you are the strongest member, and a very different thing if you are, so to speak, a weak ancillary appendix. Clearly, an appendix can go very wrong, and some people may judge that it should be taken out.

On the whole, some of us had been trying before entry, not very successfully, to imitate the French. But in order to imitate the French effectively one would have to have about twenty-five years of *École Nationale d'Administration*, i.e., the French training centre for its Civil Service highfliers. And we haven't got that here – our present system is a sort of anglicanized form of the *École Nationale*. So it is not astonishing that we were not too successful. However, one should not exaggerate the effectiveness of the French system. The French in the mid-1970s are having the same difficulties as we had a little bit earlier. This means that a persuasive plan, or indicative plan, would not work as well now without an increase in the more imperative element through a new public sector – on the lines of the Common Programme of the Left shaped when Monsieur Pompidou was in the *Élysee*, and General de Gaulle was watching over him from heaven. However, to stress the main point, there is no doubt that joining the Common Market with its very strict rules about liberalization does impinge on our liberty of action.

Of course, the problems of planning now are not simply due to the EEC. There also is the new international disorder, in exchange rates, inflation, and the recession of world trade.

One of the problems that has been under-estimated in this context is the fact that conventional statistics have given a wrong picture to the decision-makers. This has been a problem, in fact, since 1951. But it has increased in the current crisis. For instance, GNP in real terms gives a totally misleading perspective because exports and imports are valued at 1970 prices. In this way the GNP showed an export surplus even for years when the deficit was in terms of billions because the terms of trade since 1970 have deteriorated by some 35 per cent, which in terms of the national income means a real loss of roughly speaking 7 per cent – because about 20 per cent of our national income is in terms of imports. That meant that in 1974–5 there was a very sharp fall in available national resources. This very sharp fall has been bridged by an enormous amount of borrowing which, after a time, cannot be sustained.

Now I think it was very right and proper to take this first brunt of the change in the terms of trade, and the ensuing deflationary force of the immense excess of imports, by increasing borrowing. But we cannot borrow indefinitely, and it is the delayed effect of the OPEC affair – OPEC plus the general boom in commodities – which we are now beginning to pay for. I fear that it would be on the whole rash to assume that our terms of trade will improve. If there is any recovery, if the situation in Russia and China, so far as food production is concerned, remains as it is now, then we will have to reckon with a further increase in food prices. Also, possibly, if there is a recovery, say in America and Germany, we may have to reckon with an increase in some of the other commodity prices. Moreover, if the political situation in Africa deteriorates, the outlook would be even worse, because on the one hand phosphorus and fertilizers from North Africa would be very badly affected, and copper and various other metals would be very harshly affected by Southern and Middle African troubles. So that on the whole, we shall have to adapt ourselves slowly to a situation which is considerably worse, from the point of view of this country, than it has been since the War.

Big Business and Planning

Of course, there are new planning perspectives, focused on big business, and involving a considerable extension of public ownership as a planning instrument. This is partly a response to the increasing share of big business in the economy. But it also confronts the persistent view of some people that nothing much has changed in the market economy as a result of the big business or oligopoly trend.

The difficulties connected with the oligopolistic organization of industry did not arise in the last century, because the atomistic nature of competition was more or less a fact. Then the difficulties arose, because of engendering foolishly optimistic expectations, which in the end led to a slump and an annihilation of vast values. The market did not work smoothly even when atomistic competition was still existent. Now that competition over a very large field (primarily in manufacturing) is oligopolistic, coordination of investment decisions seems to me to be quite essential. I think that the hoary old argument that planners do not know very much about business really does not carry very much weight, because in most industries, especially in this country, the natural tendency is to cartelization and therefore a private coordination of investment programmes. I do not think that entrepreneurs very much object to coordination if they can do it for their own particular benefit; they object to planning because we want to do it in such a way that it will be more to the social interest rather than the private interest.

As to the market, it depends entirely on whether you think that internal and external economies of scale are important. I see that Professor Hahn of Cambridge in his inaugural lecture said the market mechanism works after all when increasing returns are smallish.[6] In this he gave a new twist to the famous dictum that, though if we do not believe in perfect competition, a large part of economic theory falls to the ground, we can always assume that the difference between theory and the real world is not very great. Let us just assume – this school maintains – that imperfect competition works like perfect competition. Then all will be well. Hahn went one better, and like the nursemaid in the classical children's book excused her illegitimate baby by saying that it was quite small. In other words, voicing a general view, he held that we haven't got much perfect competition around, but then if the deviation from perfect competition is very small, all will be nevertheless well.

Of course, such an attitude militates against the case for both planning of resource allocation, and direct instruments at the level of individual firms. But the concentration of economic power in the hands of a very few firms has certainly increased the case for such intervention, both through an extension of public enterprise and Planning Agreements with big business. I personally hope that the sort of Planning Agreement that Stuart Holland introduced into British political life will work, and that we shall have positive planning for increased investment to the point at which profits as the basis for resource allocation are a glimmer in someone's eye, but no more.

Public Ownership and Planning

I also hope that we shall be able to create a new planning capacity through taking certain key firms into public ownership. With Alfred Herbert and British Leyland, a start has already been made, through the National Enterprise Board. But I trust that a number of other key firms also will be taken over. In other areas of the economy, it is much easier to let planners go ahead in firms, for instance petro-chemicals. But in general one needs both Planning Agreements and extended public ownership. Also, one needs them in the context of an investment programme for the economy as a whole, which is basically coordinated and harmonized. Such a combination offers prospects for a positive planning process.

In such a context, it may well be worth commenting on the extent to which the Italian model of public ownership is applicable to Labour's new public enterprise proposals. With due respect, again, to my friend Stuart Holland, the Italian experience in new public enterprise stemmed from the period of Mussolini. Our position in Britain today is fortunately very

different, not only in that respect, but also in the sense that Italy
never enjoyed the resources in fuel which Britain now has, and
which – with appropriate public intervention – can very much
influence our overall prospects for planning in the economy.

However, the penetration of foreign companies into Italy has
been very much less than in Britain. In the oil sector, as a result
of the activities of Mr. Patrick Jenkin and Peter Walker and the
Conservatives, the penetration of foreign multinational capital
(in terms of the territory licensed) is about 67 per cent. Now, it
bothers me from some points of view, but I think that on the
whole the tax system that has been built up, if not perfect, is a
very important neutralizer of penetration that the Italians do
not have. We are going to take, roughly speaking, 70 per cent of
the profits on the average. I do not think it is enough, but it
is something.

Of course, there are critics of the Labour policy of a public
stake in the exploitation of oil. It is obvious – everybody asks us,
'why do you want participation?' Labour wants participation
primarily for two reasons. Reason number one is that we want to
have physical control of a large part of the oil – 51 per cent – for
national security reasons. Secondly, we must have knowledge,
and knowledge can be divided into two parts. We want
knowledge of operations, because it is nonsense to have something between 3,000 and 4,500 million tons of oil worth £50
per ton and not be able to operate an oil company. And from
this point of view, of course, British Petroleum cannot really be
counted as a national oil company, though it fields the state very
nice profits. They are first-class in finding oil and their technical
staff are admirable – the organization of the exploitation of the
Forties field is an extraordinary feat of ingenuity, and I wish
them very good luck. However, only 14 or 15 per cent of their
activity is centred in Britain, and therefore their framework is
not the framework I would like to see in the British National Oil
Corporation. That is one thing. But apart from that, the BNOC
must be able to undertake all operations of an integrated private
company – exploration, exploitation, transportation, refining
and retailing, upsteam and downstream activities, and drilling.
After all, it is not that difficult. When the Norwegians began
their experiment, they had one man and two boys and by now

they have about 200 people. They have two of their own wells, and they are doing very, very well indeed. Therefore I don't think that we should really be abashed of anything when the oil barons say that we do not need national oil companies. We badly need a national oil company, and we shall do our best to make it work.

The second thing – and this is even more important – we want immediate access to facts about costs and prices, and access to facts cannot be had if you are not a partner. That is, it cannot be had unless you wish the Inland Revenue to crawl over their books all the time, which they would not like, and I do not think it would be well done by the Inland Revenue because it is a very complicated business. You have to have extraordinarily good oil accountants, skilled in the job and well trained. For that we must have participation, and we are going to get participation, I am quite certain.

Therefore, while I do not think that we can learn much from the Italian state hydro-carbons company, ENI, except from its fearless spirit, and while I think that perhaps at this stage we shall not try to expand abroad, as they had to do because they lacked a sufficiently big base at home, we must learn to exploit our own home base fully. Whether we want to expand abroad later depends very much on how Civil Service reform is going to work, because we cannot expand abroad without experts. Nevertheless, we can learn from the Italian public enterprise experience in hydro-carbons with respect to the ruthlessness and skill of its leadership under Mattei, and his determination to show the private multinational corporations that there are public corporations which can stand up to them. In this sense of state entrepreneurship, there is an Italian example which we can well import.

8

Planning Disagreements

Stuart Holland

The failure of capitalist planning in Britain in the 1960s gave rise to two main reactions in the Labour Party. There were those who thought that such a lesson discredited commitment to any planning in a formal sense. There were others who thought that the lesson showed the need for different planning, with different ends and means for the allocation of resources in society. In other words, some held that we should plan less, or not at all, and others held that we should plan more, but with changed aims, methods, and perspectives.

This basic disagreement on the role of planning was reflected in the policy debate which followed Labour's election defeat in 1970. The anti-planners included some who held that the failure to devalue sterling earlier than 1967 caused the collapse of the National Plan with the deflationary package of July 1966.[1] This group included former ministers, such as Anthony Crosland, who anyway had held for some fifteen years that governments should not concern themselves with detailed planning decisions but, remaining 'severely empirical', should deal with the broad issues of macro-economic policy and intervene in micro-economic structures only when problems were posed by a failure of the competitive process.[2]

The pro-planners included two main groups who made temporary if strange bedfellows. On the one hand, there was a group of social democratic 'moderates', including several former and later Ministers, who were attracted by the evidence on new forms of State intervention in continental Western Europe, especially State Holding Companies and what then was known as the Programme Contracts system – a direct translation

of the *contrattazione programmatica* described by Franco Archibugi
in the Italian case, and of the *contrats de programme* as introduced
from 1968 in France and Belgium.[3]

On the other hand, there was a group of politicians on the
Centre and Left of the Labour Party who responded differently
to the same evidence on new relations between big business and
the state in continental Western Europe. While the so-called
'moderates' saw such a new State Holding Company or
companies, and new direct relations between big business
and government as secondary to conventional macro-
economic policies, the Centre and Left group within the Party –
and especially on its National Executive – saw new public
enterprise and new forms of planning as primary to any future
government economic strategy capable of transforming
Britain's economic problems.

There were three main areas of disagreement, which resulted
in a clear break between the 'mini' and 'maxi' planners – to use
Thomas Balogh's phrase. One, related to the question of a
primary or secondary role for new public enterprise and
planning, concerned the size of a new extension of the public
sector. Another was whether any British variant of Programme
Contracts – i.e. Planning Agreement – should be voluntary or
obligatory on management in the big league corporate sector.
The third was the issue of whether trade unionists in big business
in either the private or public sector – including the already
nationalized industries – should have the right to information
on and negotiation of Planning Agreements.

The first issue was polarized in mid-1973, around the
question whether the new State Holding Company proposed
by Labour – the National Enterprise Board – should take a
controlling shareholding in from twenty to twenty-five of the
top hundred manufacturing companies over a parliamentary
term, as proposed in the National Executive Committee's
Opposition Green Paper.[4] Labour's 1973 Conference endorsed
a 'substantial' extension of ownership. But it also endorsed
the proposal that Planning Agreements should be obligatory
on management in 'certainly the largest 100 or so manufacturing firms and all the major public enterprises'.[5] It
also was agreed in Labour's February 1974 manifesto that trade

unions should have the right to negotiate such Planning Agreements with big business and the government.

The New Structure of Capital

There is no doubt that there were two main reasons why the National Executive of the Labour Party endorsed so radical a programme, and why the Conference of the Party gave it such substantial support. One was the failure of the 1965 National Plan to harness the power of private capital through indicative planning. The other was related to the first: i.e. the attempt to harness trade unions and labour through a statutory incomes policy and the new legislation on trade unions through *In Place of Strife*.[6] Harold Wilson may well have regarded himself as the greatest British pragmatist since Baldwin, but the trade unions appreciated – with significant unanimity – that such pragmatism in practice meant a defensive reaction to the initiative and power of capital rather than his self-styled 'purposive' use of power in the public interest. In other words, the case for a specific strategy for economic planning was in part a reaction to the economic failure of the 1964–70 Wilson governments.

But there were further factors in the trade union and political support for new planning policies in the early 1970s. These resulted from realization of the major change which had occurred in the concentration of capital during the previous twenty years. It was appreciated by those who supported the new planning strategies that the trend to monopoly and multinational capital had undermined the assumption of competitive national firms in the conventional Keynesian policy framework. Since such factors played an important part in the debate and discussion within the Labour Party in the early seventies, they are worth specifying here.

Among the most important was preliminary evidence from the 1968 industrial census that the top 100 manufacturing companies by 1970 represented around a half of manufacturing output. This was a dramatic enough increase since 1950, when such firms accounted for only one-fifth of manufacturing output.[7] The output figures were matched by a comparable control of half manufacturing investment and employment by the top 100 firms, and implied a direct and indirect control by the top 100 companies of more than half of manufacturing pricing – in addition to the prices charged to distributors in the service sector for the broad range of manufactured goods. Moreover, it was found that the top 75 companies accounted for half of direct export trade in 1973. Besides which, the 1968 industrial census had already revealed that fewer than 75 firms represented more than half of Britain's industrial assets.[8]

In itself, this meant a new concentration of economic power in the hands of a few dozen companies which commanded half or more of the key macro-economic aggregates of the economy – output, industrial employment and assets, prices, and direct or visible export trade. It typified the transformation of the old style micro-economic models on which the Crosland case against detailed intervention at the level of individual firms and industries had been based, and its replacement by a new meso-economic sector bridging the gap between the former macro and micro economic categories.

In addition, there had been a change from predominantly national to predominantly multinational capital in the British economy in the twenty years between 1950 and 1970, with the main acceleration taking place during the period of failed indicative planning in the 1960s. By 1973 it was clear that the top 100 companies not only had increased their command of the heights of the domestic economy, but also had increasingly gone multinational abroad. By 1970, effectively, all these firms had a sizeable number of subsidiaries outside Britain, and by 1971 the value of foreign production by British firms was already more than twice total visible or direct exports from the UK.[9]

This parallel trend to monopoly and multinational capital had not only undermined the assumption of price competition between a plural structure of companies at home, but also made such firms in many cases their own main 'competitors' abroad. This meant that they had become less sensitive to exchange rate changes of the classic Keynesian kind in international trade, since following through a devaluation such as that of 1967 by lowering prices in foreign markets where they were already investing and producing would have meant reducing prices and cash flow for their own foreign operations. Granted the extent of such big business domination of Britain's export trade – with the top 75 firms commanding half of visible exports – such arguments were significant in challenging the case of those anti-planners who thought that all had been well with the 1960s save for an earlier devaluation.

Apart from this, where such British big business is not its own main competitor, it is confronted with other big league firms which would engage it in damaging price competition if aggressive devaluation-responsive foreign trading were attempted. For such reasons, plus the considerable volume and lower unit profits involved in responding fully to devaluation, British business at home has not matched the sinking pound since 1967 with dramatically falling export prices. This was related to the problem of inefficient exporting, as illustrated by a British Export Trade Research study which found that in a sample of some 220 firms accounting for a quarter of U.K. direct exports, half the firms had either no one or only one person fully responsible for export promotion in particular markets, against up to a dozen people for German and Japanese competitors.[10]

A further argument forwarded in the debate on new economic policies in the early 1970s related to the fact that in the domestic economy, fiscal and monetary policies do not bite effectively on the new big league companies. One reason lies in the fact that corporate planning for the big league spans at least five years, and often more. This is longer than the full parliamentary term of any government, longer than any chancellor's term, or his annual or bi-annual budgets. In other words, with the trend to more complex technology and longer investment planning, a divorce had arisen between the demand management orthodoxies of governments and the supply management cycle of big business. Demand management, of interest, tax, and exchange rates, still has an important role to play for the thousands of small firms in the lower and dependent half of British industry. But such firms now are mainly dependent on the extent to which the multinational big league generate investment, orders, jobs and incomes in Britain rather than abroad.

During the main phase of the postwar 'long boom', such firms had better reason to invest their relatively capital intensive activity in Western European countries or the United States, where they would be assured either of a fuller utilization of capacity or a quicker return on capital relative to a large market. Through the 1960s, the big league companies increasingly located their relatively labour intensive plant in those of the third world countries such as Taiwan, Singapore, the Philippines, Mexico, and Brazil which offer them union-free labour at a tenth or twentieth of the cost of U.K. labour.[11] With such cost differentials, plus capacity to under-state profits and avoid tax in high social expenditure welfare-state countries such as Britain, through transfer pricing, it is natural if not obligatory for the British big league to avoid investing in Britain unless the government both changes the rules of the game and promotes a higher generation of income here at home.

The Appeasement of Capital

However, if such argument carried weight in opposition, it was insufficient for them to carry the planning programme of the Labour manifestoes of 1974 into government policy in office.

At the 1973 Labour Party conference Tony Benn had stated to acclaim from the platform that 'the crisis which we inherit will be the occasion for fundamental change and not the excuse for its postponement.' The new claim was based substantially on the extensive trades union support for the new planning powers endorsed in Labour's Programme 1973, and partly on the basic simplicity of the new policies themselves.

For instance, both further public enterprise in the form of the proposed National Enterprise Board and the Planning Agreements proposals amounted to harnessing the power of the newly dominant big business in the heartland of the economy. When so much of the economy was commanded by so few firms, it could well have appeared feasible – despite the opposition of some of the older generation parliamentary leadership – that the impending crisis following the OPEC oil price rises would harden ministerial minds in favour of positive reaction to transcend the crisis rather than to submit yet again to the receding tide of capitalist confidence.

Yet a year later, at the 1974 Labour Party Conference, Harold Wilson was able to argue that no government could have foreseen the scale of the crisis that Labour inherited in February that year. He explained it – there and elsewhere – in simple terms: the inflation of raw material, commodity and oil prices meant that Britain, like other countries, had to pay more for her imports. Higher import prices would meant more inflation of prices on the domestic market, since firms would have to pass on the cost increases in price increases. To 'solve' the crisis, we would have to cut back our own consumption, hold back wages and export more. Price controls and food subsidies would cushion the impact of the new, short-term inflation.

Almost before the conference was over, business interests began a sustained campaign against price controls, corporate taxation levels, the rate of wage increases, and the level of public spending: They argued that ceilings on price increases meant they would be caught with inflated costs and lowered profits. They discovered – for the first time – that the book-keeping exercises they had used for time immemorial meant higher tax due on profits declared for stocks in hand (as their price and sale value rose). They maintained that profits and investment would collapse unless price controls were relaxed, tax relief given on stock appreciation, wages controlled, and public spending cut.

At the same time, the government found that the Treasury book-keepers of our national accounts had lost effective control of public spending and accounting. Local authority programmes had been cleared for some years past on the assumption that their costs would be covered from tax receipts in the expanding economy. The public sector borrowing requirement, basically the borrowing which the Treasury had to ensure to cover public expenditure, increased to levels which were considered 'unacceptable' to foreign holders of sterling. Pressure was put on the government to draw the teeth from the radical parts of Labour's Programme 1973 and the 1974 manifesto commitment.

For a while the government tried to be all things to all men. In other words, it tried to mediate between capital, its pressure

groups, and its political representatives, and labour and the
TUC. Its balancing act was not simply a matter of personalities,
or the 'trade off' politics of the Prime Minister. It needed to
appear to balance, or mediate, both to placate capital at home
and abroad, and to avoid offending the unions during the
period in which the £6 wage deal was negotiated.

This appearance of nominal independence between relatively
equal power groups in society has been an increasing feature of
postwar politics in the mature capitalist countries. But it can
only last for so long as the economic system itself 'produces the
goods' for the power groups themselves. In the sustained 'long
boom' of the postwar recovery, governments were able for the
most part to manage taxation and negotiate wage guidelines
which gave both capital and labour increased returns.
Governments appeared able to 'manage' the economy in broad
terms.

The breakdown of sustained expansion posed a challenge to
Labour in government, and to the leaders of the trades union
movement. The challenge was that of essentially alternative
strategies for coping with the crisis. It would be solved either on
capital's terms or on labour's terms.

Capital's terms amounted basically to 'solving' the short-
term crisis in the economy by restraining wages, relaxing the
price code, lowering taxation, cutting public expenditure and
making room for profits. Labour's terms, as spelled out in
Labour Party policies for planning, meant 'transforming' the
long-term crisis of British capitalism, of which interrupted
expansion and inflation were only a part.

In practice, the government edged closer to the capitalist
'solution', and drew the main part of trade union leadership
with it, however reluctant that leadership and however genuine
their misgivings. In successive budgets and major policy
statements it has ceded the four main demands of the capitalist
case: wage restraint, relaxation of the price code, lowered
taxation, and public spending cuts.

The pattern of negotiation of the £6 and $4\frac{1}{2}$ per cent wage
deals is well known. The relaxation of the price code
accompanied the July 1976 expenditure cuts of £2 billions,
which themselves followed the £3 billions cuts in planned public

expenditure increases in earlier Healey budgets. The estimated increase in employer's insurance contributions of the July 1976 measures, nearly £1 billion on paper, hit labour not capital, since employers in fact were allowed to 'pass on' the increased charges in higher prices under the relaxed price code. The previous measures of tax relief on stock appreciation, in themselves, have been estimated as amounting to a £4 billion indirect subsidy to the private sector over the three years from November 1974 (through not charging them that amount in tax). By the end of 1977 only about a tenth of some £20 billions tax on capital and income came from the corporate sector rather than from personal taxation.[12]

Such a package represents a virtually unparalleled shift of resources from labour to capital by any postwar government. For the labour movement it represents a complete reversal of the strategy of the 1974 manifestoes. It has undermined the legitimate expectations of thousands of Labour activists, and those of millions of voters who may have been sceptical of the Labour leadership but nevertheless expected Labour in government to put up a significant fight for its policies.

More importantly, from the government's viewpoint, the failure to intervene effectively on the level of investment, output, employment, or prices undermined the basis of the so-called social contract between the trade unions and the government. This agreement in principle has been differently interpreted by different beholders and actors in the drama of Labour in government in the 1970s.

For some former Labour ministers during the February 1974 election campaign, it amounted to a *carte blanche* commitment by the unions to undertake a 'voluntary' wages policy, thereby appearing to give a new lease to the incomes policies which had been discredited in the 1966–70 period, not least with the fiasco which followed the defeat of the trades union legislation *In Place of Strife*. For some leading trade unionists it meant a commitment by the government both to implement the new industrial strategy of the Labour Party and to repeal the Conservative industrial relations legislation, which had already imposed heavy fines on some unions.

Whatever the lack of clarity, the failure of the government to make any serious attempt to implement the industrial strategy undermined the basis for maintaining a third year of 'voluntary' wage restraint under the Social Contract framework. When the government failed to give powers in the 1975 Industry Act to either the National Enterprise Board or Planning Agreements system – making acceptance of them both 'voluntary' rather than 'obligatory' for big business – it thereby undermined its capacity to harness the power of meso-economic enterprise in a planning framework.[13] Its appeasement of capital meant a one-sided contract.

The result was an increased confrontation between the Labour government on the one hand and the main part of the Labour movement on the other. The Labour Party and TUC conferences from 1975 through to 1978 passed resolutions demanding obligatory Planning Agreements with the top 100 companies, and major new powers for the National Enterprise Board, with spending powers of at least £1,000 millions a year. But the union leadership itself in the TUC remained uncertain of the extent to which it could pressure the government for implementation of the planning strategy of the Labour movement itself. When faced with confrontation on the government's 10 per cent wages rule through 1977–8, it supported the government rather than groups of workers in the public sector who had largely been left out of the previous Heath 'threshold' or index-linked wage agreements.

Political Resistance to Planning

If one stayed within a liberal capitalist framework of analysis, one might interpret the failure to implement the new planning strategy as 'lack of will' or 'lack of understanding' (either of the fundamental nature of the crisis of the economy, or the need for equally fundamental policies to transform it). In fact there is little doubt that such subjective factors played a part in the divorce beween left-wing theory and capitalist practice in opposition and in office respectively. Some of the leading former members of the government between 1964 and 1970 lacked the will to take real account of the shortcomings of indicative planning in the sixties, and transcend them with real planning powers in the following decade. A few of them were more concerned to justify their efforts at previous forms of intervention by reincarnation in mummified form a decade later.

Thus Harold Wilson as leader of the opposition tried to veto the National Enterprise Board proposals when they were first made by a sub-committee of the Labour Party's National Executive, and worked hard to ensure that the new State Holding Company created in 1975 looked as similar as possible to the previous Industrial Reorganization Committee. Similarly, Denis Healey made a statement of so-called industrial 'strategy' in November 1975 which effectively took the proposed tri-partite debate between government, management and unions back into the NEDC seminar framework, and away from the workshop of company board level where it could have been given real power.

Some other former ministers appear never to have read the new industrial policy proposals for the NEB or Planning Agreements elsewhere than in the columns of a hostile press, and to have run for cover as soon as they were misrepresented there. Thus Roy Jenkins stated on television that he was in favour of a State Holding Company with selective shareholdings in enterprise, but not in favour of 'dogmatic nationalization' of the kind envisaged in the NEB proposals, apparently not realizing that the Party's proposals were for a State Holding Company with controlling shareholdings, very similar to that which he had himself earlier proposed in a series of major speeches.[14]

However, such factors in the divorce between policy and practice are secondary. Essentially, those who opposed the new Labour Party planning policies knew very well what they were doing. While confused on more than mere detail, they nevertheless realized that the policies – if implemented in the new commanding heights of the economy – would represent a fundamental and probably irreversible shift in power away from private capital in favour of labour.

More specifically, such a challenge to the freedom of private capital to determine the basic outcome of investment, output,

employment, prices and trade would have given rise to major
questioning abroad – both in the United States and in the
various representative institutions of capitalist government on a
global scale: multinational companies themselves, and
international agencies such as the IMF, EEC, OECD, etc. Thus
the appeasement of capital and the vain effort to regenerate
investment and jobs through the seventies was a placating not
only of capital itself, but also its first line institutional defences
abroad.

The Radical Planning Rationale

Certainly, the degree of radicalism in the new policies was not
seriously in question to those involved in or following the
debate within the Labour movement from 1972 through to
1974, even if such radical change was demanded more by the
facts of crisis and the patent failure of the previous Keynesian
orthodoxies rather than a return to fundamentalist principles.

First, there was the relation of the economic strategy in
Labour's of the Programmes to the previous analysis of the
specific features of fundamental crisis in British capitalism. The
debate in the Labour Party in the early seventies was focused on
the extent to which the liberal capitalism of mainly small scale
national capital had been transformed by the monopoly-
multinational trend. In effect, the case adopted by the National
Executive in 1972 and 1973 endorsed the view that there had
been a trend to monopoly and multinational power which had
divorced key elements of the Keynesian macro-micro synthesis.
The advocates of the case stressed the extent to which the newly
emerged power structure amounted to a change in the
dominant mode of production, distribution and exchange
which necessitated a fundamental change in thinking and
policy, especially regarding public enterprise and planning
controls.

Second, the policies for new public enterprise and new forms
of planning via (inter alia) the National Enterprise Board and
Planning Agreements, were framed in this context. They
stressed the extent to which manufacturing industry was crucial

for export trade (some 85 per cent of direct exports) and regional development, yet showed that there was a shrinking manufacturing base in Britain related to excessive capital outflow abroad. Their advocates admitted that technical progress means the displacement of labour by less labour intensive investment, but argued for this reason that the maintenance of full employment in Britain would involve both a broad wave of new investment for social use and a planned distribution of its location. They underlined the fact that the first generation nationalizations had brought mainly basic industries and services into state ownership (rather than social control), and underlined the fact that the nationalized industries, with the exception of coal and steel, were unexportable, and could contribute little to gaining command of the national balance of payments. In short, key features of the productive and unproductive sectors case, plus the tradeable non-tradeable distinction later publicized by Bacon and Eltis, were familiar themes in Labour's planning debate before 1974.[15]

Third, the analysis in opposition of the unequal mix in the so-called mixed economy identified the fact that while public expenditure had already outstripped more than half of total spending, public enterprise (or the supply versus the demand side) represented less than 20 per cent of the total value of goods and services in the economy. It was emphasized that virtually no public enterprise was represented in the key manufacturing sector, save where salvage operations (such as Rolls Royce) had brought in enterprise by accident and the unwillingness of the private institutions to venture its so called risk capital. With the recognition of the fact that indirect intervention would not mobilize sustained investment and modernization in the private manufacturing sector (whether by budgets or indicative plans), this constituted one of the primary cases for a major extension of new public ownership through the main industrial sectors as the basis for reversing the previous imbalance between private and public economic power.

Fourth, the case for Planning Agreements, or strategic controls over leading companies, was strictly related to the premise of new public enterprise operating through the main manufacturing and service industries. In other words, it was not imagined that legislation or formal requirements alone could harness the concentrated power of the new giant enterprises to socialist objectives. The case for 20 to 25 leading firms to be brought into the National Enterprise Board over a parliamentary term was founded on the premise that without such a penetration of the dominant monopoly-multinational sector, both direct action and indirect leverage on investment, output, prices, jobs, and trade would be necessary – through a new public power structure – on the remaining private enterprise in the big league sector. Analytically, this can be seen as the case for transforming the dominant private mode of production in the big league sector with means for a new dominance of public power through ownership and planning.

Fifth, none of this was undertaken in ignorance of the nature of state power in capitalist society. It sought to transform the relations between capital and labour through a major extension of economic power for labour both within enterprise and within government. A key dimension to this analysis was the case that trade unionists should have the right to disagree with, challenge, and change, the decisions of management in both private and public big league corporations through negotiating Planning Agreements on their future plans up to and into Whitehall. The potential transformation of state power which would be opened by trade unionists actually negotiating the changed direction of use of resources in companies commanding half economic activity was evident enough. This was especially so granted that such direct trade union bargaining on the deployment and use of resources was to involve shop stewards from the companies themselves, elected on terms decided within the enterprise by its workers, rather than national or regional union officials alone, or unionists amenable to and appointed by ministers.

Union Roles versus Union Rule

One reason for the failure to translate the radical planning policies of opposition into planning in government certainly lay with the hesitation of the trade union leadership to demand the 'full bill of goods' on industrial policy in return for the first two years of wage restraint through the social contract.

Again, as on the political and government side, this may in part have stemmed from an incomplete grasp by some leading trade unionists of the need for 'maxi' planning, with real powers, to cope with the economic crisis, defend employment, and preserve public spending. But, as also at the level of political and state power, trade union leaders were aware of the scale of opposition from big business, its organized pressure groups, and the press and media.

Probably, however, the specific hesitation of the unions related to more general factors. Put simply, British trade unionists – like most counterparts abroad – have little desire to rule rather than to exert a key role in the negotiation of economic policy, and to defend the general interests of their members as a class within society. In such ways they hesitate as much as capital itself to become patently involved in government responsibility for the specific allocation of resources.

In one respect this is not surprising. The February 1974 general election had been fought by Edward Heath and the Conservatives very much on the real or imagined issue of 'who rules'. Labour's majority after the October 1974 general election was slim, and later to be eroded. In addition, the divisions in the Parliamentary Labour Party and the determination of the Wilson cabinets to resist the force of the Programmes placed the unions in an invidious position. Their insistence early in the lifetime of the government on 'the full programme' could have resulted in no wages agreement, a transparent split between government and unions, and coalition pressures from the Right of the Parliamentary Labour Party which, with a slim majority, could perhaps have resulted in a 1931 setback for the Labour movement as a whole.

Not least, in such circumstances, a general election could have reversed Labour's position as the largest single party and resulted in a Tory government bent on reversing the new Employment Protection Act, which itself had reversed the Conservatives anti-union legislation of the early 1970s. By insisting on one further step forward, the trade union leadership could conceivably have found itself forced several paces back to a position where it could with difficulty fulfil even its conventional role.

Certainly this was not the whole picture. Despite a nominally left-wing President, there was a power vacuum in the second largest union in the country, the engineers, following a trend to the right in the election of its General Secretary and a nominal majority of one vote against the 'Left' on its executive. Besides which, there was the role of the shortly to be out-going Labour Prime Minister. Harold Wilson's departure lacked all save the epitaph of Louis XV. After him the economic storm broke with a vengeance. Before his acceptance of the garter there was a period in which his pronouncements to different interest groups were difficult to reconcile with reality. Thus he talked of the National Enterprise Board as 'the greatest leap forward in economic thinking and policy since John Maynard Keynes' – which even its authors could dispute – while shortly thereafter delivering an Industry Bill gelded of any real powers.

Besides which, the TUC did not in fact let up in its own advocacy of the 'full programme'. The TUC Annual Economic Reviews for 1976 and 1977 demanded compulsory Planning Agreements with the top 100 companies by 1979, which is a radical demand if the agreements are to represent a change in the planning of the companies which command half our output and more than half our export trade. The demand is still 'on line' with Labour's Programme 1973, and underlies the reaffirmed demand for such policies in Labour's Programme 1976. They also demanded, in the same document, that the National Enterprise Board should be allocated resources of £1 billion a year (equivalent to a third of recent manufacturing investment) rather than the £1 billion outright which the government so far has granted, most of which will be swallowed by British Leyland alone.

Planning and Economic Power

It would be superficial to claim that this represents nothing more than the difference between pretension and reality in the

Labour movement. There quite clearly is a high degree of sensitivity in the TUC economic committee to the need for the 'full programme' as a minimal condition for the regeneration of British industry in the context of national planning. This is quite apart from the vocal minority (including new recruits to radicalism such as NALGO) who have opposed the moderation shown in actual TUC bargaining with the government.

The present situation is different from that of the 1960s in the very existence of a detailed Labour Party strategy which can meaningfully be described as socialist; the extent of continued TUC support for that strategy as a medium-term policy in its own policy statements, and the direct involvement of the TUC at the highest levels of government decision-making.

If TUC involvement to date has been passive rather than highly active, it must partly relate to the lack of a mass campaign within the Labour movement in support of the 'full programme' of the Labour Party. Trade union leaders are elected on different terms, with different degrees of recall and accountability. Nevertheless, many are responsive to a greater rather than a lesser degree to their base. And partly as a consequence of the short period between the publication of the full form of Labour's new economic programme in the summer of 1973, and the general election in February the following year, there was little time in which a major debate between leadership and base on the merits of the programme could be mobilized. By the time that trade unionists at shop-floor level were alerted to the significance of the Party's economic programme, the Labour government had undermined the obligatory revelation of information and the right to bargaining in Planning Agreements which was its principal attraction to the shop floor.

Meanwhile, the fundamental structural crisis of the British economy proceeds virtually unchecked. Since 1973 we have seen an interrelation between specific forms of crisis such as the OPEC oil price increases, and the underlying crisis of de-industrialization and unemployment. The post-1973 crisis is not an accidental, once-off and soon-to-be-reversed problem arising from oil sheiks alone. The trend to unemployment through technological progress, an imbalanced visible trade structure through multinational capital, and inflationary price behaviour in the big league firms would have hit Britain in the mid-1970s irrespective of the commodity or oil price inflations of the decade. The underlying imbalance between public enterprise and public expenditure, tax receipts and reverse tax handouts, plus longer supply cycles with shorter term budgets, would have posed economic crisis for Labour in government now for precisely the reasons identified in the shaping of the Labour Party's strategy for the seventies.

These structural problems – part general and part specific to the British economy – cannot be solved by holding back wages, cutting public expenditure, and making room for profits. In fact the government will impose a further disincentive to capital to expand output and investment in Britain by the scale of its cuts in public spending, 80 per cent of which goes straight back to the private sector in the form of demand for goods and services.

Meanwhile, in its capitulation both to capital itself and to the financial orthodoxies of the IMF, two Labour governments composed predominantly of social democrats have presided over the biggest attack on the fabric of the welfare state – through expenditure cuts – in recent history.

Of course, North Sea oil, and its impact on both sterling and the balance of payments by the end of 1977, had given the Labour government an advantage. It raised the value of sterling, reduced import prices and the domestic rate of inflation, and increased reserves. On the other hand, these gains on the sterling and payments front mask the underlying structural crisis of the economy which have already been described both in the British context and in nominally better structured economies such as West Germany. The problems of structural unemployment, stagnant investment and ineffective demand will stay on the horizon. The importance of a planning strategy for the structural, social, and spatial redistribution of employment, output, and income will remain undiminished if governments have any ambition to command the economy rather than merely occupy office.

Generalizing the lessons from the anti-planning experience of Labour in the 1970s, it becomes clear that the new planning policies shaped in opposition between 1970 and 1974 both challenged the then dominant ideology of Keynesian liberal capitalism, and gained majority endorsement through the conferences of the Labour Party and the TUC. What they failed to assure was the translation of these policies through from political opposition to the level of state power.

Two main factors other than the trade union role were important in this rejection of planning. One was the power of the Civil Service and state apparatus itself.[16] The other was the power of the Prime Minister and the appointment of anti-planners or 'mini-planners' in a majority of the Cabinet posts from 1974. In themselves such oligarchic concentrations of power not only are strikingly in contrast with the pluralist model of democracy favoured in textbook theories of checks and balances, but now are being challenged by campaigns within and outside the Labour Party itself. The right of Ministers to organize the work and personnel of their departments themselves, rather than submit to the dictates of a committee of Permanent Under-Secretaries and the Civil Service Department, has been advocated forcefully by a working group of the Conservative Party. The right of the Labour movement to elect its own leader, rather than delegate it to the Parliamentary Committee, and increased pressure for accountability and re-selection of Members of Parliament, has been a feature of the debate on internal party democracy in the Labour Party in the mid-1970s, partly reflecting the dramatic divorce between theory and policy, or Party and government, in the same decade.[17] Pressure to elect the shadow cabinet and Cabinet – on Scandinavian lines – from the whole Party rather than partly from the Parliamentary Party and on the Prime Minister's whim – is likely to follow.

Such reforms towards accountability and election would go a long way in the democratization of economic power. We are supposed to enjoy a political system in which Parliament is the sovereign political power, and in which the state intermediates between the claims of capital and labour. In a real sense this assumption parallels the premise of the model of consumer sovereignty, whereby the consumer is served by an enterprise which draws upon the capital and labour markets in serving consumer needs and requirements.

In practice the reality of both economic and political power is very different. Under conditions of monopoly domination of the main markets in the economy, producer power is sovereign, subject to the dictates and criteria of capital, and largely imposing its decision on what should be produced, why, where, how, when, and for whom on both labour and the consumer. Similarly, the central relationship in the modern capitalist economy is between capital and the state, and especially between big business and the Civil Service. Capital largely imposes its terms of operation on both government and labour, while the government in turn imposes its own demands – almost exclusively – on Parliament.

Mr. Callaghan's simple message to the 1977 Labour Party Conference – 'back us or sack us' – speaks volumes for the subjection of parliamentary parties in few enough words. Parliament is denied a scalpel and offered an axe. In such circumstances it is hardly surprising that parliamentary parties of the Left hesitate to press for planning rather than submit – however unwillingly – to the range of compromises which governments make with capital under the veil of 'national interest'.

If the labour movement, in Britain or elsewhere, is serious in its pretension to transform a capitalist mode of production and to introduce mechanisms for democratic planning, it would seek to reverse the central domination of resource allocation by capital and the state and to establish the dominance of parliamentary sovereignty and the institutions of the labour movement at the heart of the system of power. In such a reversal, Parliament would and should remain sovereign in relation to the trade unions, granted the greater legitimation of its legislative power through the general electoral process. But the primary responsibility of a majority of the Left in parliament would be to labour rather than to capital, and to the transformation of the use of resources from private to social criteria through the mechanisms of democratic planning.

Similarly, at the level of industry and enterprise, any serious approach to the democratization of economic power would represent a reversal of the dominance of capital and management over labour into a dominance of new elected representatives of labour, with the power to hire and fire management, and to take part in the negotiation of changed criteria for the use of resources by enterprise in a planning framework. The hire-and-fire power has been well enough illustrated to be practical in the Yugoslav case, even if the Yugoslav experience indicates that in leading enterprise of the meso-economic type it is crucial for central government to determine the criteria and direction for the use of resources in the last instance.

With the reinforcement of consumer representation through the institutions of a democratic planning process, the main conditions of consumer sovereignty in goods and services could be re-established. As importantly, through a planned and socialized used of resources, the interests of other groups of workers and consumers, on a regional or sectional basis, could be legitimately taken into account through their own direct representation in the planning process.

If the dominance of social and public criteria for the use of resources was established within enterprise in such a socialized mode of production and distribution, the finance for key projects and services through the economy could be democratically negotiated through the planning process on social use value rather than the private exchange value of capitalist enterprise. In this sense it would represent finance for enterprise rather than capital in the classic sense.

Such conditions for the democratization of economic power will be essential premises of any advance beyond capitalist resource allocation or new attempts at capitalist planning of the indicative kind. The feasibility of such an advance will depend on a variety of factors. These will include the extent to which the parties of the Left are able to demonstrate the unviability of modern capitalism under conditions of trend to structural unemployment, public expenditure restraint, wage controls and price inflation. But such a negative critique of the crisis in modern capitalism will not be sufficient in itself. The dominance of capital's power in the contemporary economy depends substantially on the continued hold of a dominant ideology of liberal competitive capitalism in an era of monopoly capital power. It also depends on the extent to which governments and media continue to maintain that the problem of national economies in crisis depends essentially on labour, wage costs, and industrial practices rather than global under-consumption compounded by the erosion of national sovereignty through the rise of multinational capital power.

In this sense, the issue of the dominant ideology is crucial to the feasibility of transforming the dominance of capital over the state, and of reversing the state's oligarchic dominance over Parliament and democratic institutions. This implies two dimensions to a political strategy – at the ideological level – for the Left: (a) exposure of the myth of predominantly national and price competitive capital serving the public interest; (b) a campaign to legitimize new public intervention for socialized development through democratic planning.

Jaques Attali, in this study, has already raised the problem of legitimating an alternative mode of development. Jürgen Habermas also has argued forcefully that the capitalist state was posed with a crisis of legitimation – even before the incidence of the specific form of economic crisis in the mid-1970s, following the commodity and oil price increases and the deflation of public spending and demand by Western European governments.[18]

What has emerged in general in the mid-1970s has been recognition of a crisis in Keynesian ideology, and with it – implicitly – a crisis for what can be called the Keynesian social democratic state. The vacuum was filled in Britain, not by the counter-case for socialist planning of *Labour's Programmes* 1973 and 1976, but by Friedmanite, pre-Keynesian monetarism. Governments through the main OECD countries have appeared to follow Friedman's case for cutting public expenditure, reducing public enterprise or running it at cost rather than social cost benefit lines, and decreasing personal taxation. The emphasis on balanced budgets has consequently imposed beggar-my-neighbour deflation on Western Europe.

It appears to have mattered little to the new monetarist ideologues that Friedman himself never recommended incomes policies, while wage restraint has been a key feature of the government counter-inflation policies. Nor has it appeared to concern governments that in their return to an economics which is both pre-planning and pre-Keynes, they have neglected major changes in the structure of international capital which have transformed the European economy since the 1930s. In practice, capital has gained its terms for crisis 'resolution', based on a reduction of spending, employment, and wages of a kind which will only aggravate the crisis of effective demand and spare capacity.

Political Legitimation

Politically, in some countries, pressure from parties and trade unions will be necessary to counter this capitalist attempt to resolve the current crisis. In other countries, the parties nominally of the Left may underwrite or endorse such policies through lack of conviction in the viability of the socialist planning alternatives. But in the French case, the elections of March 1978 have been indicative of the force of public opinion in favour of a change of direction towards socialist policies. There is little doubt that the period of some five years between the formulation of the *Common Programme* of the Left and the political divisions emerging in September 1977 registered an important impact on persuading wide sections of the electorate of the need for change in the economy and society. The results of both rounds of the elections, when the combined parties of the Left registered around half the total vote, are remarkable in view of the formal disunity of the parties themselves on what the specifics of the *Programme* should mean, and the scale and pace of change which they should entail. Rarely, in recent history, can such a vote have been gained by several parties so resolutely divided between themselves.

Thus there is a considerable case for claiming that five years of debate, discussion, and advocacy of fundamental change registered a profound ideological impact on the French electorate – changing, confirming, or enlarging the public's view of the feasibility of change itself.

In Italy, a similar credibility of change from Christian Democratic oligarchy, and the case for democratization of the economy, was gained by the Communist Party in the early 1970s. This followed a long period of conscious effort in building consensus support for a change in the exercise and use of state power, along essentially Gramscian lines. Whatever the view of the ultra-Left within Italy, or the Left abroad, of the limits of the PCI's position, there are strong grounds for maintaining that the consensus building undertaken was for change rather than for the management of Italian capitalism by an alternative party.[19]

Put differently, while in the short term political disagreement on planning may appear negative and a denial of progress, the medium- to long-term impact of the case for change can result in a fundamental shift in attitudes on the feasibility of change itself. Ideology, in any real sense, involves not only ideas, but also presumptions, assumptions, unstated premises, and plain prejudice about the running of the economy and society. It involves in a real sense what people consider 'legitimate' in both politics and policy.

Change, reversal, or transformation of a dominant ideology legitimating capitalism is unlikely if capital itself is delivering the goods and services to which the electorate as consumers have become accustomed. But it becomes feasible in a period of crisis in which the goods delivered are at astronomic prices, to consumers who already feel the need for qualitative improvement in their social and physical environment. It is potentially more credible in a period of high unemployment and inflation in which the goods are not delivered at all to broad sections of unemployed and those reduced to a subsistence level by inflation.

Clearly, the raised conviction on the need for change may come from the Right rather than the Left. In crisis, myth spawns on unemployment and inflation. But the example of the French case – despite the result of the second round of the March 1978 elections – should lead those on the mainstream Left and Centre to see the feasibility of mass support for a strategy for socialism. Not least, the criticism of key features of the policies of governments nominally of the Left by parties of the Left mainly gain rather than lose credibility for the parties as agents of change.

In this sense, the following two chapters of this volume may serve the purpose of illustrating that there is a convergence of thinking and policy across international frontiers on the Left. Critics of the 'utopianism' of the proposals which they represent could take account of the extent to which the policies recommended for democratic planning are already on the agenda of major parties of the European Left. If their translation from theory to policy has yet to occur, or if better policies are to emerge, this is substantially up to the combined forces of the Left itself.

PART V

International Potential

9

The International Crisis
*Franco Archibugi, Jacques Delors
and Stuart Holland*

Inflation and Crisis

Inflation has become a problem of dramatic proportions. At the
national level, it encourages economic speculation, provides
some people with unjustified profits, and results in a generally
unjust allocation of income, especially when the direct and
indirect income of certain social groups (in particular, the non-
active sections of the population) are not adjusted in line with
increases in the cost of living.

Inflation constantly distorts the assessment of economic
performance and frustrates rational calculation in both the
public and private sectors. Inflation thus contributes to a less
rational distribution of the factors of production. Savings are
moved out of long-term investment into forms of 'hedging'
against inflation (precious metals, land, etc.) or are kept in
liquid form, simply not reinvested. As a result, inflation alters
the terms of lending and the criteria for choosing investments,
thereby wasting resources or reducing growth potential and
creating higher structural unemployment.

Further, the implementation of anti-inflationary measures
which concentrate unduly on single aspects of the problem such
as reduction of the public sector borrowing requirement have
given rise to substantial distortions which have often meant that
public authorities have to sacrifice plans for structural reform
and public services.

The overall effect of inflation is to jeopardize progress
towards a more egalitarian society; to aggravate social tensions

and intensify the corporatist reactions of those wanting to safeguard acquired privileges; it thus erodes democracy.

At the European level, the differences between rates of inflation and the specifically national character of anti-inflationary measures face the European Economic Community with real prospects of disintegration, accentuated by the present conditions of international competition and by the 'beggar-my-neighbour' policies of a number of member countries, which prompt others to give priority to their bilateral relations with the United States. Such developments make a Community response to inflation even more unlikely.

The dramatic increase in the pace of inflation in the 1970s was due to a combination of circumstances: namely, a particularly sharp economic upturn in all industrialized countries, accompanied by rapid cost-push and demand-pull inflation; an explosion in raw material prices due partly to overheating and ancillary factors such as the use of oil as a political weapon; and an acute phase in the upheavals besetting the international monetary system.

However, this is only part of the story. These accelerating factors – both cyclical and quasi-accidental – occurred against a background of *structural inflation rooted in profound economic, social, and political changes which have occurred in the last twenty years.*

Forty years ago, Keynes formulated the main elements of a new economic theory based on the principle that, if public authorities intervened to regulate private and public demand, the price mechanism and competition would ensure a supply of goods and services at full employment without inflation.

Since then, there has been a considerable change in the general economic framework. The widespread use of demand management, full employment, and welfare state policies has considerably altered the pattern of both public and private spending.

In the meantime, our economies have been subject to the rapid growth and increasing influence of very powerful large firms described here and elsewhere as the *'meso-economic'* sector, a new phenomenon between micro-economics and macro-economics. This sector does not respond to overall demand management by the public authorities in the same way as an economy based on small firms. The structure of competition itself has been transformed and operates under new 'rules of the game'.

The combination of stagnant investment, rising unemployment, and persistent inflation since the late 1960s indicates that the regulation of overall demand alone as advocated by Keynes is no longer in keeping with meso-economics. To cope with these new factors, the Keynesian approach needs a new and different complement, transcending the orthodox macro-micro dimensions of economic policy and planning. Besides this, several key assumptions on which European integration was based have been profoundly modified.

It frequently is neglected that the report of the Spaak Committee (1956), which preceded the Treaty of Rome, stressed that considerable imbalances and inequalities could *result from* the liberalization of foreign trade, capital and labour, a warning that was reiterated ten years later in the Community's first Medium-Term Economic Policy Programme.

Although the Community has now implemented the main points of its trade liberalization programme and its programme for the free movement of workers, the progress envisaged and achieved in the structural areas of sectoral, regional, and social policy has been limited or insignificant. This is now classically apparent in the failure of a Community response to the structural factors in inflation, which cannot be isolated from economic, social, and political factors. For instance, a number of measures that brought very positive social benefits, such as those for ensuring better job protection, for providing assistance to farmers, and for narrowing income disparities, have played their part in fuelling inflationary pressures, for want of a coherent general framework of policies for coherent development.

There are two main ways in which governments could master inflation: either accept recession and depression resulting from over-reliance on traditional instruments of economic policy, i.e. '*stop-go*' *measures*; or undertake a *programme of more fundamental reforms and measures within a new planning framework, designed to achieve a more balanced economic, social and political structure.*

In order to halt inflation, 'stop-go' measures would have to be applied more frequently and on an increasingly wider scale, with intolerable human and economic cost, now less and less acceptable and causing a greater waste of resources. If full employment, a better distribution of resources and the profits for investment cannot be safeguarded, measures which simply restrict demand will increasingly clash with social expectations of improving the quality of life, extending public services, combating inequality, promoting individual liberties, achieving a higher degree of participation and social integration, etc.

The public will not tolerate these contradictions for long. Therefore, unless far-reaching reforms are undertaken, there is a great danger that authoritarian methods – open or concealed – may gradually obtain a hold on our democratic societies.

Meso-Economic Power

Macro-economic demand management policies assume that competition determines price formation at the micro-economic level. In other words, it assumes a price-flexible supply and demand in response to monetary and fiscal policies. This fails to take into account the emergence of a new 'meso-economic' sector between the macro-economic level of public policy and the micro-economic level of small and medium-sized undertakings. (Greek: mesos – intermediate.)

The term 'meso-economic' refers to the *increase and growth of monopolistic, multinational companies*, whose behaviour is totally different from that of small-scale national firms in the micro-economic competitive model, and which constitute a new economic sector between the conventional macro- and micro-economic orthodoxies. The structure of competition itself has thus been transformed. What has emerged is a new dualism between large and small firms (meso-economic and micro-economic undertakings).

The following figures illustrate the size of the meso-economic sector:

In the United Kingdom, less than one per cent of firms

account for 50 per cent of the country's output and foreign trade. 100 firms control half of industrial output, with 75 firms accounting for half of direct exports and 31 firms for 40 per cent of direct exports.

In France, the top four firms in each of the following industries accounted for over half the total sales in 1969: metal-working (82 per cent), extraction and processing of various metals (80 per cent), steel (77 per cent), aircraft construction (65 per cent), production of non-ferrous metals (60 per cent), oils and fats (54 per cent), rubber and asbestos (52 per cent).

In Germany, about 2·5 per cent of industrial firms accounted for more than half of total sales in 1968.

More dramatically, in the EEC Nine as a whole, some 332 companies now account for half of industrial sales. Moreover, while Britain shows a more concentrated industrial structure than other Community economies, the rest of the EEC are 'catching up' in terms of both monopoly market structures and multinational spread of capital.[1]

There is every indication that meso-economic firms are continually increasing their share of the market despite the policies attempted at national and Community levels to maintain plural market structures of the old-style competitive model.

The growth of this powerful new meso-economic sector is not a conspiracy against the public interest; it is the natural outcome of economies of scale and the need for specialization. Its monopoly trend is a consequence of competition, not simply an abuse of the competitive process through collusion.

However, the inflationary power to raise prices is in part a direct result of the rise of meso-economic power: there is a significant correlation between the size of a firm and its ability to set its prices at a relatively high level, thereby earning super-normal profits.[2]

In the new meso-economic sector, consumer sovereignty has been replaced by a producer sovereignty, by which the new big business can 'impose' prices. Large firms generally set their prices in relation to the costs and prices of smaller marginal firms. This provides a kind of *price umbrella* for those small firms which large firms, or public authorities, want to keep in business.[3] This policy enables competing firms of very different sizes to remain on the market and offeres the more viable firms super-normal profits which, in turn, makes possible their further expansion and unequal strength relative to 'micro'-economic competitors.

The price umbrella technique now has been extended to trade between subsidiaries of multinational companies in different countries, i.e., using the *transfer pricing* technique. These companies can thus promote inflation by raising the prices of imports from their foreign subsidiaries virtually with impunity.

The price umbrella practice is substantially the perverse result of competition policies which encourage price increases instead of curbing them. Large firms set their prices at a level which permits a number of competing firms to remain on the market (an objective of competition policy).

This practice is inflationary in that: it makes for a constant upward alignment of prices; it slows down the process of modernizing equipment and thus narrows the scope for subsequent price cuts. This does not mean that competition no longer exists. In fact, meso-economic firms both continue to compete for a larger share of national or world markets, and at the same time enter into various types of agreement designed to limit other effects of competition and strengthen their own position as firms. In short, large firms are motivated in different and more complex ways than conventional economic theories suggest: they aim as much to expand their activities and supplies and markets, as to raise the profitability of their operations; the ultimate aim, in terms of power, is survival and relative autonomy. But, in this battle, *price* competition has increasingly been suspended – both between big business in the meso-economic sector, and indirectly between it and the micro-economic enterprise of the conventional model. *This has affected the relationship between productivity, returns, and prices in different sectors.* Industrial growth has been rapid but unequal both among sectors and regions. Productivity, therefore, varies considerably between sectors and among regions. The fact that increases in productivity differ from sector to sector is not in itself inflationary, provided that the most productive sectors pass on to their customers a considerable share of their gains in the form of lower prices.

However, the sectors in which productivity gains are the most rapid rarely reduce their prices: high-productivity sectors, which are dominated by a few leading firms, can conduct virtually independent pricing policies regardless of their productivity. As a result, profits and wages in these sectors will rise sharply. Given the general tendency to pay equal wages for the same type of work, higher wages quickly spread to other sectors of the economy. Sectors in which productivity increases at a relatively slow rate raise their prices even more sharply in order to be able to pay the higher wage rates and ensure their survival. In brief, *the greater the productivity differences, the greater the increase they now can entail in the general level of prices.*

Besides which, the structure of profit margins in the distributive trades is generally such that measures taken to hold back prices, particularly in industry, often do not work through to consumer prices. There are a number of reasons for this, including: traditional and outdated structures in part of the distributive trades; the gradual replacement of price competition by a form of competition which tends, on the contrary, to raise costs and prices and involves in particular artificial differences in products, markets, prices, and related services; massive, insistent, and largely emotive advertising; prestige goods and items 'for show'; the 'middle class' bias policy pursued by many governments; the low price elasticity of demand on many markets (inadequate market transparency, lack of time available to consumers, particularly as a result of the increase in the number of women who go out to work); growing consumer expectations regarding choice of varieties available, presentation of products, product specialization, etc. Also, more generally, in the new consumer society there is a tendency for prices to be related to the satisfaction *expected* from the purchase or possession of an object, or from the use of a service – social prestige, attempts to imitate or to be different from others, etc.

This is very much related to the middle-class bias of government policies, or general concern to placate professional and managerial élites by allowing them income levels which cannot be achieved by the working class.[4]

The size of the distributive trade's profit margins in terms of consumer prices can be illustrated by the following statistic: the gross trading surplus of the distributive trades alone is equivalent to about half of the gross trading surplus of industry as a whole.[5] In a number of countries, the distributive trades' surplus is even larger than that of industry.[6]

Among other factors, the main reason for this is that traders often calculate their selling prices by adding a fixed percentage to their cost prices. Wherever demand is relatively inelastic, this is tantamount to indexing profits to cost prices. This triggers primarily an upward pressure on prices. A downward movement in producer or import prices is rarely passed on to the consumer Moreover, the development of integrated retail outlets often has little beneficial effect on consumer prices. Although, at the outset, supermarkets and the like frequently apply a policy of low prices in order to attract customers and to drive small competing traders out of business, they then often raise their prices, thereby making considerable and unwarranted profits. In addition, their advertising and promotion techniques frequently disguise long-term price increases.

Labour, Capital, and Crisis

The Treaty of Rome provides for the free movement of workers within the Community. However, it has now been widely shown and recognized that imbalanced geographical migration is extemely costly in social and economic terms and thus fuels inflation.

Generally speaking, *the factors making for an inflexible supply of manpower are not dealt with rationally.* This is a matter of fundamental importance. It goes a long way towards explaining shortcomings in public policies. Inflexibility is often the result of undeniable social progress which no one would think of reversing, e.g., laws and agreements on job security (length of notice of termination of employment, accident prevention, redundancy payments), improved benefits for the wholly unemployed, the creation of opportunities for promotion within firms, etc. There also is increasing attention to demands that a certain level of employment be guaranteed in the less favoured regions of the Community when the major employer in a town or locality announces a cutback in production.

However, granted the social and economic aims of modern society, it would be a mistake to reject the aim of achieving improved allocation of manpower. In this respect, although the active employment policy pursued since the last war has produced very positive results, its limitations have, since 1965–8, become apparent to differing degrees in the countries concerned.

One of the main new problems, of which governments have taken little or no account, is the long-term trend to structural or technological unemployment in the main economies of the Nine. The postwar boom into the mid 1960s was sustained by the absorption in entirely new industries of labour displaced by technical progress in traditional industries. But since the mid-1960s, increased product and productivity in even modern sectors of industry has been matched by a falling rate of growth of employment. Without a new generation of job-creating industries on the horizon, and with a trend for technical progress (e.g. in micro-electronics) to substitute machines for labour in the service sector, classic full employment policies are thrown into crisis.

Related to this is the *inability of certain groups to obtain worthwhile employment*. This is the case for handicapped workers or foreign workers who have lost their previous jobs, but there is also an increasingly serious problem for the elederly, the ever-growing number of women seeking their first jobs or wishing to return to work after raising their children, and school-leavers either with qualifications for which there is no demand or with no real vocational qualifications. This has led to an increase in structural unemployment, even during phases of rapid growth.

Even when a large number of young people and women were registering with employment exchanges, firms were complaining of the shortage of skilled labour, which led to outbidding on the wages front between firms in need of such labour. The steps being taken to extend adult training schemes are not an adequate answer to such problems posed by shortage of skilled workers. It also should be stressed how difficult it is for some employees to move to a new region: the arduous business of selling their homes, which they often own, and of buying another in a new locality; the fact that such a move does not always fit in with the occupation of the spouse, who cannot always move as well; the loss of certain indirect wages or work advantages, although here collective agreements have resolved a number of difficulties; the inadequacy of the social infrastructure (schools, hospitals, transport facilities, etc.).

All things considered, even under conditions of overall job expansion, employment policy has failed to create the conditions necessary for a voluntary mobility that is satisfactory from both a social and an economic viewpoint. There are other causes such as the lack of a genuine market for part-time employment, which clearly would help adjust labour supply and demand in particular areas.

This criticism in no way implies that an attempt should be made to reverse the gains already made by trade unions which are, in any case, irreversible. However, *a comprehensive review of employment policies* that also makes allowance for the limitations of medium-term and long-term forecasting in this field is called for. Only a radical *redistribution* of the structure of employment, between firms and industries, regions and cities, and different social classes, will be able to fulfill the classic ends of postwar full employment policy in the remaining decades of this century.

The allocation of capital is also subject to considerable rigidities, although financial capital is much more mobile than individuals.

Leading firms (meso-economic firms) – through price-making power – have more scope today for maintaining their profit margins and sales in periods of depressed activity; as a result, a key feature of the conventional price and profit mechanism is no longer functioning. But, for the same reason, self-financing now is a regular feature of their capital-raising. Therefore, leading firms have relatively less recourse to the capital market. This is one of the causes of fluctuations in capital markets in recent years, but is a main cause of the declining role of stock markets.

Inflation is accentuating the tendency among firms to raise capital by issuing bonds rather than shares. This is an important aspect of the general trend away from share issues, prompted, in particular, by the systematic extension of interest rate subsidies offered by central or local authorities and by the desire of firms to avoid control by institutional investors (banks, insurance companies, etc.) in countries where these have large shareholdings.

This increasing recourse to bonds for raising capital creates another inflationary factor, since it leads firms to maintain or even raise price levels in a recession in order to meet their fixed interest payments, and cover their higher unit costs (with spare capacity) through inflation rather than increased sales. This has transformed the price sequence of the conventional trade cycle. Previously, prices rose during the upswing of trade and fell in the recession. Nowadays, prices rise in *both* the upswing *and* the recession.

Moreover, this tendency is aggravated by government stop-go policies. The more a government relies on a policy of restricting demand, the more firms tend to raise prices in order to compensate for the drop in turnover resulting from the fall in sales. Thus deflation can *cause* inflationary pressure.

Such factors are not unique in the current inflation in the EEC. Nevertheless, it is notable that the average rate of price inflation in the Nine effectively doubled in the decade 1964–74, i.e., before the major increase in commodity and oil prices caused governments to impose deflationary domestic policies to make room for higher raw material and fuel costs.

It is in the post-1974 situation that the new deflation-inflation syndrome has become critical. Overall, inflation rates have decreased in some countries, such as Britain and France, as the main initial impact of OPEC and other price rises have diminished. These dis-inflationary effects have been reinforced in an economy such as Britain's by wage restraint policies accepted by trades unions. But, over the longer term, only a comprehensive reflation of demand, related to public policies for effective price control in the meso-economic sector, can ensure that leading firms decrease prices in line with the reduction of their unit costs of output through higher sales.

Moreover, there is no guarantee that such policies will prove effective if governments attempt to reflate demand without a fundamental change in its structure and distribution, essentially moving public expenditure from a secondary and passive role to a *primary* and *active* position in the socially planned allocation of resources. This is partly because of the psychological shock of the crisis of the seventies to management confidence that further major investment projects could be covered by sustained private demand, and partly from increasingly apparent limits in a mode of development based primarily on private consumption and investment.

Private versus Social Consumption

Spurred on by advertising, consumption in our society tends towards a model which includes a large measure of frivolous, ostentatious or, at the very least, non-essential consumption. There are several factors behind this: anarchical advertising; artificial differentiation of markets, models, prices, and related services (guarantees, after-sales service, etc.); unnecessary changing of models; production of over-sophisticated and expensive items in place of simple, more efficient and cheaper goods; insufficient consumer information (comparison of prices, technical characteristics and durability of products, etc.). Tied to this pattern of consumption, a society based essentially on private consumption tends to consume too much too quickly. This generates heavy pressure for increases in direct and indirect income, while demand, despite the prices charged, expands too rapidly, spurred on by a supply of goods and services which are of increasingly questionable utility and novelty.

None the less, consumer demand today also is increasingly concerned with the 'quality of life and working conditions': it concerns needs, some of which could be organized or provided publicly (housing, public transport, cultural and social services, etc.) and others privately (organization and content of work, desire to keep occupational expertise up to date, greater worker participation, and increased industrial democracy). In general, these problems are poorly perceived both by public authorities and employers. Both prefer to try to solve disputes and ease tension through traditional negotiations on wages and working hours. Such an approach fails to solve the problems involved, and at the same time boosts inflation in the following respects. Increased wage costs are passed on by firms in the form of price increases. The unduly heavy pressure of consumption (resulting from the increase in direct or indirect incomes) limits the resources available for 'social investments', which do not receive the necessary priority. Production costs are aggravated by absenteeism, high staff turnover, and poor quality work, all of which reflect wage earners' frustration with their working conditions.

Public policy in this connection shows four main expenditure trends:

An increase in subsidies to meso-economic firms rebating and negating nominal corporation tax.

A growing share of tax transfers or social subsidy in the structure of household incomes.

An increase in goods and services acquired with public subsidy (direct or indirect) in traditional private consumption.

An increase in goods and services provided 'free of charge' in enlarged private consumption.[7]

Public transfers, and in particular social security transfers, are obviously an integral part of the policies aimed at achieving a fairer distribution of national wealth and income and attaining the fundamental objectives of improving social welfare and cohesion.

In most cases, direct income demands are formulated in such a way as to take account of the transfers which must be made to the state, but do not allow for cash payments or public services provided by the public authorities. A substantial inflationary pressure begins to weigh on costs, especially during wage negotiations. This is one of the conclusions to emerge from an OECD study of expenditure:[8]

. . . it seems clear that the rising tax burden stimulated

income claims . . . and was thus one factor tending to keep up
the household sector's share in 'primary' incomes. How far,
on the other side, the rising volume of transfer payments
(many of which go mainly to the aged, sick or unemployed)
helped to mitigate claims for higher money incomes is an
open question. . . . These questions . . . lie at the centre of
the process by which resistance to attempts to shift the
distribution of expenditure away from 'pure' private
consumption generates inflationary pressures. . . .[9]

Secondly, the Community countries do not yet have a
breakdown showing to what extent national product is used for
meeting the various needs of society (education, health, social
security, research, law and order, housing, recreation, etc.) and
to what extent the various sectors (public authorities, firms,
households) contribute to meeting these needs.[10]

In the absence of such an overall survey, it is impossible to
evaluate fully how growth contributes to meeting these needs.
Endless political discussions take place without a sufficiently
extensive and coherent statistical base. In such circumstances, it
is very difficult for the public authorities to make rational
choices and to fomulate coherent policies.

While the public authorities can allocate part of new
resources to new objectives, it is extremely difficult for them to
cut back previous allocations. This therefore results in *a highly
rigid structure of public expenditure*. Thus, the utilization of the
national product has not been sufficiently adapted to the
changing needs of society. The inadequacies of social
infrastructure in general and of public transport in particular
are striking examples.

As has been seen, these inadequacies give rise to 'qualitative'
demands for which satisfaction is sought – with little success – in
conventional wage concessions (direct and indirect) and which,
in their turn, fuel inflation. These contradictions will become
even more marked if, as everything would tend to suggest,
growth over the coming years stays below the rate of the
immediate postwar decades.

All in all, the present, conventional economic model leads to clear dilemmas. Having failed to make the necessary policy choices, policy-makers continue to maintain personal taxes and equivalent charges in order to be able to step up transfers, subsidies, social welfare schemes, etc., neglecting the effective corporate taxation which would become possible through a reflation of demand and a change in the model of consumption. This then creates tax-push inflation, the various aspects of which have been studied in depth by the OECD. Moreover, the level of personal taxation in several member states is reaching the bounds of what will be tolerated with impunity. If the option is made for a lower level of taxation, a choice also must be made between the following alternatives:

to slow down the development of public services, thereby increasing the sense of frustration in society in the short-term;

to finance it peversely (i.e. expenditure not covered by taxation);

to introduce or increase direct contributions to the cost of the services by those using them;

to stimulate savings so as to increase financial resources;

to cut 'welfare state' services and reverse the social advance which they have represented in the postwar period.

Crisis in Policy Formulation

After the Second World War, growth was a prime objective of economic and social policy. It was unquestionably instrumental in recovering employment and raising living standards. But it also promoted the internal strains in the economic and social systems of our countries. Since these strains were not in due course eliminated, they produced inflationary effects.

Inflation is therefore not only a source of increased distortions, but a sort of flight away from present realities. It masks certain structural problems and temporarily eases certain strains, but at the same time lays the foundation for even more serious tensions leading to social and political crisis.

Foremost among these problems and strains is the persistence of *considerable inequalities of income and wealth.* The differences between per capita income in the various regions of the Community have not appreciably narrowed in the sixties, and widened in the seventies.[11] Certain groups of workers have further consolidated their direct and indirect advantages, while others (small and medium-scale farmers, small traders, certain categories of wage earners) have seen their relative situation deteriorate. Economically unwarranted gains have become larger and more common (property speculation, earnings of certain professions, investment income, and middle-class hedges against inflation). Certain new forms of unjustified profits have developed (dividends received by the shareholders in large meso-economic firms who make little, if any, contribution to financing investments and who do not incur significant risk, even in periods of marked recession). At the same time, conspicuous consumption has become increasingly common, highlighting these inequalities and reinforcing the general desire for parity.

Even in countries with a strong trade union structure and a relatively high social consensus, there is a marked tendency to decentralize the decisions in which trade union organizations are involved. This tendency is reflected in the greater strength wielded by both management and unions in business, and in a greater awareness and often even greater willingness at grass roots level to take steps on matters which concern them directly.

Decentralization is not a bad thing in itself – quite the contrary – but its success depends on the ability to combine greater initiative at the base with a necessary minimum of coherence of action at the top. However, this is occurring less and less, in some countries not at all. Consequently, employer-employee relations become more and more uncertain, agreements and contracts are drained of their value, and the only possible solution to the problems of industrial bargaining is to be found increasingly in inflation.

Besides individual trade unions, some countries have for a long time had organizations representing particular groups of the working population (farmers, small traders, craftsmen, civil servants). In recent years these groups have also adopted new, much more aggressive attitudes. In most countries, specific groups have recently set up their own representative organizations and are resolutely applying all the means of pressure at their disposal. This is a new and complex form of corporatism operating at all levels of society.

These two tendencies (decentralization and corporatism) have led to social groups competing more keenly between themselves. This competitiveness is becoming more and more compartmentalized. This makes it virtually impossible to carry out the redistribution effort on a general basis. The danger of this corporatist tendency is all the more serious since it is not countervailed by policy-makers, who should be the guardians of the general public interest. In some countries, renewed awareness of the cultural and linguistic identities of regions is further tending to compartmentalize decisions.

Given these tendencies, political decision-making has never been so necessary. But, substantially through a crisis in ideology, based on the attempt today to recreate the conditions of yesteryear, it lacks either intellectual credibility or political force.

The fundamental principles underlying most political institutions and procedures were conceived years ago in very different economic, social, and political circumstances. These circumstances have altered profoundly. Institutions and procedures have not adapted to these changes.

Social and political objectives have become many and varied. Their relative importance varies considerably from country to country and from one interest group to the next. The hierarchy of objectives is vague and their interrelationships not at all well understood.

False Relationships

Thus, many discussions on economic policy are still dominated by the explicit or implicit assumption that close relationships exist between several objectives, particularly between prices and costs on the one hand, and unemployment and the balance of payments on the other. These relationships are in general much more flexible than is supposed. Where they exist and hamper the fight against inflation, they can often be loosened by a change in the behaviour of the main power groups in economic activity.

The relationship between prices and employment, which even in the past presented different characteristics in different countries, has changed appreciably in recent years; the slower creation of new jobs has led to an increase in the 'structural' aspect of unemployment. In addition, structural factors – including the rise of meso-economic price-making power in big business – have had an ever greater effect on price trends. It now should be obvious that the conventional 'cyclical' relationship between prices and unemployment has virtually been reversed. If governments stick to conventional policies in order to curb inflation, they will vainly apply increasingly rigorous restrictive measures. Because of the ability of large firms to set their own prices, deflationary measures can actually reinforce inflation, as firms increase prices to offset a fall in demand and thereby maintain or increase cash-flow. The resulting social costs result in increased social tension which is the more serious precisely because governments appear to misunderstand its basic causes and fall victim to secondary mythologized explanations of crisis such as monetarism.

The situation is aggravated when it comes to the relationship between prices and the balance of payments. According to conventional theory, a balance of payments deficit should prompt governments to implement a restrictive monetary and fiscal policy (and vice versa). But when a currency is allowed to float without any state intervention, a balance of payments deficit no longer necessarily has the same restrictive effects on overall demand. Responsibility for managing the foreign exchange position passes from the central bank to private finance. The system becomes increasingly unstable as it is taken out of the hands of the authorities. Consequently, the deflationary and reflationary relationships between prices and the balance of payments are undermined, thus encouraging inflation.

In many cases, the phenomena previously described have led to decentralization of public decision-making and a diversification of social structures. But this tendency towards more direct democracy has not been accompanied by adjustments of socio-political structures sufficient to offset the neutralization or negation of central state power.

Consultation and negotiation procedures between interest groups in society are proliferating, overlapping, and being drained of much of their value. In many cases, the very object of consultation has been defeated by the *multiplication of procedures*, unrelated to a central strategy for the use of economic resources.

In addition, several old-style rules and constraints have, in reality, disappeared: wage-productivity alignment, the balance of payments constraint on domestic expenditure, and other international monetary 'norms'.

These difficulties are further aggravated by the *weakness of political decision-making*. This is partly due to the narrow margin between majority and opposition parties or defensive government effort to achieve consensus within majority parties. These are factors which reduce the room for manœuvre available to parties in office, since they tend to result in lowest-common-denominator tactics rather than a strategy for basic change, including a change in the mode of development. Such factors partly explain the weakness of the political parties, the instability of governments, and the difficulty governments have in taking major economic and social decisions. This is in addition to the divergent economic interests previously described which weigh more and more heavily on processes of political decision-making, to the point of paralysing them.

These phenomena are the outward manifestations of a profound transformation in the way democracy works in our countries. Some of them are positive; but the institutions have not been adapted to new ideas or new realities, with the result that increasing difficulties are encountered in coordination and decision-making.

Under these conditions, inflation substitutes for the failure of other instruments to mediate and adapt claims to real and objective possibilities.

10

Planning for Development
*Franco Archibugi, Jacques Delors
and Stuart Holland*

It has been argued that the current crisis of the Western
European economies is fundamental and structural, rather than
cyclical and short-term. It reflects major changes in economic
power, not least the rise of dominant big business in what has
been called the meso-economic sector, and an undermining of
the relative influence of the modern capitalist state on economic
activity. It also reflects general changes in private consumption
demand for consumer goods at prevailing levels of unequal
income distribution, and a trend to technological unemployment in even the 'modern' sectors of activity. The
crisis is both ideological and political.

This crisis in ideology and democratic power relates therefore to structural problems inherent in a far-reaching
transformation of the market economy and society. These
changes, some of which have in fact generated major social
advances, particularly in conditions of employment and social
security, have not been accompanied by new up-to-date
methods for analysing or managing the social side of the
economy which, by introducing different means for democratic
control and distribution of growth, could transform the present
crisis through a new mode of planned development.

Effective action against structural unemployment and
inflation must, therefore, work towards two objectives. A
transformation of the postwar model of growth into a new
model of development, which in turn will demand new
perspectives for predominantly social rather than private
allocation of resources, with an extension of social versus

private consumption. This calls for urgent action at national and Community levels to deal with the behaviour of meso-economic firms, in the structure of supply of goods and services, the formation of prices, in employment and in capital markets, where they now occupy a dominant position.

The achievement of such a new model of development will in part necessitate new economic and social planning based on a coherent and democratic choice of priority social aims; a permanent but flexible system of social negotiation for change – in particular extending the role of trade unions beyond conventional bargaining on wages and working conditions, whose terms of reference are established at present by public and private capital.

It would be foolhardy to try to put forward immediately any miracle solution to these problems, which would amount to nothing less than a social transformation. Nevertheless, the main elements of such a transformed mode of development are clear, and could be implemented at Community or national level, with varying degrees of intensity.

Redefining Economic Strategy

If our society is to tackle structural unemployment and inflation effectively over the long-term, it is essential to make and to adhere to a coherent strategy for society and the means of achieving it. This means major changes for our institutions. The success of such an effort will depend essentially on changed relations between the three main economic and social actors in the present system: government, the trade unions, and the business organizations. It must concern the following new dimensions.

A widening of the scope of negotiations between those involved in economic life, both in terms of content and of those who participate in negotiations. With regard to the content, it is important to take into account not only the role of the direct income of the parties involved (wages and profits), but also distribution (unearned income), indirect factors (taxation, transfers, community services), and qualitative factors (working hours and conditions, decision-sharing within the firm);

A democratization of decision-making, between central and local government, employers, and trade unions;

A new institutional framework for negotiation of change, grouping together government representatives and professional and trade union representatives. It should be made obligatory at least to consult with such a body, though the views expressed by its members on the main options of short- and medium-term economic policy need not be the same;

A reinforcement of the primacy of political debate and a widening of political decision-making. This implies the strengthening of parliaments, which should be put in a position to make the main decisions concerning society;

A new planning framework to help the representatives of the relevant social groups to implement choices once made. The bodies officially or unofficially responsible for preparing the technical ground for planning could make better use of their role and experiment with more effective forms of dialogue and negotiation. Without it, they will be condemned to the preparation of forecasts, lacking the capacity to implement real change itself.

A New Model of Development

Fulfilment of a new model of development will be subject to a number of fundamental constraints.

First, the choice between various aims in our societies. At present, governments and the main social pressure groups call at the same time for a continuing increase in material living standards, an improved quality of life, more social equality, more autonomy, and more public involvement, etc. Some of these objectives clearly must be given precedence over others.

Second, achievement of a new model of development will have to be a *long-term process*, since it will require far-reaching changes in the structure of production and employment. However, the pace of adjustment will probably be faster and more dramatic in the years ahead. This will increase social risks and disrupt accepted attitudes, especially as growth is likely to be slower in future. New methods will have to be established to ensure that such changes can be made without jeopardizing the objective of full employment; for instance, a reduction of the working week with an equalization of the right to work.

The new model cannot be developed in isolation from the global economic and monetary framework, the considerable uncertainties stemming from the need for a new international division of labour, from the struggles between countries over the distribution of wealth, etc.

These trends will raise difficult problems for government economic management: reshaping the pattern of consumption, investment, and competitive capacity, renegotiation of the distribution of employment, etc. The solution to these problems can only be found through new forms of planning, for change of the economic system, with new processes of democratized negotiation for change.

In such a new model for the development of society, greater attention must be paid to the qualitative factors which increasingly determine real welfare: increase in leisure time and leisure use, improvement of working conditions, protection of the environment, and changes in public intervention (e.g. public transport versus private transport).

It is therefore essential that the public's desires and needs should be more fully understood and represented. The information supplied by the market must be supplemented and corrected by other means, such as surveys and polls; development of social indicators, etc. An increasingly large proportion of national product should be used to meet these needs, reallocating resources and making choices as necessary.

This new emphasis on qualitative factors will mean that there will have to be a reallocation of national product. This in fact is in line with adjustments which anyway have been made necessary by recent events – the fundamental aim being to curb the increase in certain types of expenditure to free resources for other expenditure, to produce the exports required to offset the recent rise in the cost of some imports, and to provide aid to developing countries. These changes will call for a major reorganization and social control of the structure of production. They must be accompanied by action to align the structure of incomes with the new social pattern of production.

As regards *private consumption*, steps must be taken to promote the production of goods of better quality and durability, fight against artificial obsolescence and to curb the overall increase in private consumption in the medium-term. Such measures – which in aggregate should be offset by an increase in *public* consumption – should include:

stimulation of personal saving and in particular medium-term saving;

review of certain forms of bank lending and consumer borrowing, including credit cards, etc.;

review of certain selling techniques, such as mail-order selling, tie-in sales, etc.;

reduction of superfluous advertising not only on a voluntary basis, but also through organizing corrective and comparative advertising, etc.;

curbing certain specific types of consumption (i.e. those which endanger health, spurious innovations of the 'me too' variety;

no longer relying on tax measures alone to reduce consumption;

organizing and extending consumers' rights through protection of health and safety; information and education and consultation and representation.

As regards public *sector consumption* (and social transfer payments), the necessary reforms must be carried out to make measures in the field of health, social security, education, etc, more socially effective.

As regards *investments linked directly to production*, the aims must be to:

promote the investment required to carry out the structural adjustments made necessary by changes in relative prices, in particular in the field of energy and raw materials, the new international division of labour, etc.;

promote a more stable pattern of economic growth related to the objectives of social use and consumption, negotiated through new planning procedures focused on big business in the meso-economic sector;

use taxation and greater selectivity in the granting of credit to discourage over-investment and the innovation for its own sake associated with the practice of model differentiation and 'planned obsolescence';

possibly create a Swedish-style investment fund into which companies would have to pay part of their profits, and from which the resources could be freed only after consulting or obtaining the agreement of the trade unions.

In the field of public-sector expenditure, given the emphasis being placed on qualitative factors, priority must continue to be given or be restored to social and human investment and services, despite the fact that this entails greater operating expenditure than public investment in purely economic infrastructure. For one thing, such public and social services have in many cases been neglected or run down relative to private consumption. Further, the expansion of social services is a key area for long-term absorption of a workforce which cannot be assured industrial employment under conditions of displacement of labour through technical progress.

Also, the key criterion should be the quality of the service rendered to the population and not simply the financial cost of the investment. The investment and the operating expenditure required to put it to full use should be treated as one cost. Orders for social infrastructure projects should be undertaken in the context of a planned restructuring of resources. Interrelated projects must be planned jointly, both to cut the cost of the investment and to enhance the service provided (e.g. coordinated policy for public transport, housing and town planning).

In order to ensure that public investment schemes (especially in recreation and the arts) provide an optimum return in terms of social use on the funds available, account must be taken when selecting and planning such schemes of the views of the public who are the potential users of this infrastructure. Through direct exchange of information and representation, working people themselves should be able to determine what facilities they want and need, where and when. Such steps must be taken if all sections of the population, and in particular the least well off, are to reap real benefit from new schemes to promote social leisure and cultural infrastructure.

Structural, Social and Spatial Change

As already indicated, *employment policy* must be reconceived to take account of the trend to technological unemployment in industry and the lack of entirely new labour-increasing industries on the present technical horizon.

This should involve a redefinition of the right to work, transcending either the pure market right of workers to offer their labour to employers on what terms they can find, or the general right of 'full employment' implicit in the welfare state commitments of the postwar period. The structural unemployment trend now makes plain that not all labour can be fully employed indefinitely, at whatever wage.

Technical progress in some industries could ensure a forty-hour week plus overtime for some workers, but would entail permanent or quasi-permanent unemployment for others. Lower wages for labour in general would not guarantee full employment, on the macro-economic side, through an implicit reduction of effective demand in the economy as a whole, with its disincentive to expanded investment and productivity.

Employment policy therefore should be reconceived in a social context, in which the gains from productivity no longer accrue mainly to capital, with the costs paid by the labour unemployed. If technical progress is to prove a boon to society, rather than a bane for individual groups of workers, its benefits through raised productivity should be more equally distributed through society as a whole. This involves both income and jobs.

On the income side, public policies should focus on the redistribution of income gains from productivity between industries and other sectors of activity. This would involve new dimensions to fiscal policy, transcending not only the present vain subsidy of private profit by public money (through non-taxation or tax remission) but also a selective tax policy, with different incidence in different sectors of activity.

Incomes and jobs are clearly interrelated. With advance on the side of productivity and its redistribution, it would be conceivable to reduce working hours, days or weeks in the year while assuring increases in income to labour. Similarly, with a reduction in necessary labour time in individual branches of activity, more people could be employed both in the individual sectors concerned and in other sectors of activity financed through the re-distribution of productivity and income through the system as a whole.

This *structural* dimension to new policies for employment and productivity clearly implies a major *social* redistribution of income between different social groups and classes. This should entail two main dimensions.

First, what is known as the social wage could be increased beyond the minimum conditions established in unemployment benefits, family income allowances, supplementary welfare benefits, etc.

Second, the concept of a basic minimum wage should be enlarged to a policy for a basic minimum *income*, both for wage earners and for those who are unemployable because of disability, age, etc.

The macro-economic feasibility of specific increases in these social and personal incomes will relate to the degree of progress possible in specific countries through new forms of planning and social negotiation of change. In this context, the maximal impact of a minimal number of meso-economic enterprises makes feasible a coherent degree of planned relationships between productivity gains and income distribution.

In addition, these structural and social dimensions to change should be related to the *spatial* distribution of gains from change between regions and urban areas, including concentrated unemployment in inner cities.

The structural change entailed, and the regional and urban distribution of a balanced employment structure, will clearly necessitate a relative change in the balance of public and private power in resource allocation. New intervention, spearheaded by public enterprise in the manufacturing or 'transformation' industries will probably be necessary to offset private capital's investment hesitation and preference for central area locations.

Experience has shown that the scale and nature of regional aids available (subsidies and transfers) are insufficient to reduce persistent regional differences. Their impact on location is minimal, certainly in the case of large firms in the meso-economic sector which are best equipped in management terms to establish new industries in less developed regions.[1] The budgetary cost of such ineffective intervention also adds to inflation inasmuch as the available funds are often wasted, for example, on the large firms which need the least assistance. Meanwhile, the reduction of effective tax revenue acts as a disincentive to government reflation. Such measures can be fully effective only if they are part of a direct and selective planning of investment with specific quantitative objectives.

The ideas outlined above may seem inappropriate in the present climate of recession. However, the preconditions for recovery should not be obscured by the immediate and damaging short-term features of the present crisis. It is for this reason that 'reflationary policies' should break new ground and be based on a new approach to development, new consumption patterns and new dimensions to social policy. Now is the time to prepare the way for a future development pattern that is more consistent and less anarchic, more socially just and less inflationary, especially granted the fact that the traditional remedies have proved so ineffective and so incapable of combating the combination of inflation and unemployment.

Planning for Change

The present frequently oligarchic and literally élitist processes of decision-making in society are largely unsuitable as a framework for implementing the above recommendations, and in practice tend to inhibit or obstruct them. If progress is to be made in changing the model of development, parallel changes must be made in the access of interested parties to decision-making on change itself. This would mean not only an enlargement of the area for negotiation of change to include wider trade union involvement, but also an enlarged role for representation of consumer groups, regional and local representatives, and so on.

Such access will only be effective if it is based on both a widening of existing information, restricted at present to governments, and the elaboration of new forms of social and economic accounting.

This elaboration should be three-dimensional and parallel the analysis of the case for change itself. In other words, it should be *structural*, *social* and *spatial* in content. It should aim to provide not only a new scenario of the possible, but also create the framework for actual change in the use of resources in a democratic planning framework.

The various parties involved in negotiation – including government, management, and unions – should be given every opportunity to obtain information about the methods of analysing and evaluating data already available, and help to determine priorities for enlarging the scope of national accounts and other statistics.

The new disaggregated accounts should cover the following:

social consumption and investment;
a cross classification of production – particularly of national product – by function and economic category;
incomes broken down by category, economic sector, socio-economic group and income bracket;
regional accounts;
accounts of real and financial assets;
welfare indicators.

The performance of large firms and multinational companies (the meso-economic sector) should be represented as a new and supplementary dimension to both existing national accounting categories and to the additional categories proposed above.

In terms of such standard categories as production, investment, employment, imports, exports, etc., this should mean an identification of the individual meso-economic enterprises responsible for half of the macro-economic totals, with a disaggregation by individual sub-sectors. Similarly, the new social indicators should be co-ordinated with and related to existing conventional national accounts.

These new 'enlarged' accounts should be made available as a term of reference in wage negotiations and trade union negotiation on working and social conditions, as well as national negotiation of economic policies. This should include annual budgets and medium-term programmes in order to assess performance against objectives: e.g., direct income (before and after taxation); social transfer payments, public and social infrastructure, increased leisure time, the reduction of inequalities, improvement in the quality of life and working conditions; the accounts of central government, local authorities, and social security institutions in order to coordinate their activities and thus eliminate duplication, waste and the inappropriate allocation of resources in relation to the objectives pursued; plus the various negotiations about social conditions including employer – trade union agreements.

Not only should the scope of negotiations between government, management, and unions be enlarged (by quantifying qualitative aspects as far as possible), but the main objectives and their interrelationships should also be specified and integrated into 'reference tables' to provide a coherent accounting framework.

These new terms of reference should take account of the following factors:

the interrelation of productivity, production, capital employment, absolute and relative prices, returns to factors of production and unemployment;
the interrelation of the revenue and expenditure of public authorities (including local authorities), disposable incomes, and the allocation of national product by function and sector;
the interrelation of the financial resources of the various sectors (variation in their commitments and claims), the monetary base, and exchange rates.

Each table would imply a choice between several basic aspects, e.g.:

investment-labour ratios, productivity gains, etc.;
public or personal distribution of productivity and income gains;
production at home or abroad in one region or area rather than another, etc.

The tables should also include general norms or guidelines on utilization of national product by sector and region; public revenue and expenditure; the public-private sector mix.

These tables could be used for forecasting future trends and preparing alternative strategies. They also could show clearly the consequences of attaching more weight to one specific objective and demonstrate how it can be attained. Once several alternatives had been prepared, the next step could be the choice of a 'target,' implementation of the target and, if necessary, its adaptation to take account of later changes. As the support of public opinion is essential for the success of the policies proposed in this report, it is important that the public be informed regularly and objectively. This is difficult because of the natural inclination of the mass media for sensationalism and over-simplification, as well as the trend towards fragmented interest groups, quite apart from the defensiveness of governments who neglect the ultimate dependence of their own effectiveness on consensus public support.

There is a clear need for the allocation of resources and means for more information and better education on economic matters for broader sections of the population, as well as for those making major decisions affecting economic and social developments. The public should also be better informed about the work and decisions of parliaments.

More specific proposals could include an annual parliamentary debate representing different views on the extent to which economic and social development corresponded in practice to the objectives which the new process of democratization and negotiation had established; the publication of income, wealth, and tax returns; the transformation of indirect subsidies into selective direct subsidies, whose scale and extent should be published, plus a Social Audit on the role of big business in the meso-economic

sector in contributing to or falling short of the new planning
objectives.

Planning, Negotiation, and Agreement

The abovementioned activities are just as important at
European as at national level in cases where the following
factors are involved:

(a) Community assistance and aid to big business;
(b) mergers involving firms in two or more Member States;
(c) information on the activities of multi-national companies,
      including inter-subsidiary trade.

Institutional arrangements and procedures should therefore be
adapted and developed with this in mind. For example, a
committee of representatives of employers' organizations and
trade unions should be set up to advise the Commission's
Directorate-General for Competition on restrictive practices
and further ways of containing multinational firms more
effectively.

*In other words, it is a matter of bridging the gaps in the means of
intervention of individual member states and opening the possibility of
intervention at the relevant Community level, i.e., extending effective
sovereignty rather than imposing a supra-national policy for its own sake.*

It is in the interests of economic and social balance and
dynamism that there should be a sizeable number of small and
medium-sized firms. However, it is becoming increasingly
difficult to set up viable firms of this type, let alone keep them in
business. Keeping marginal firms in business artificially, a
policy pursued for different reasons and to differing degrees by
meso-economic firms and the public authorities, is a definite
cause of inflation.

The viability of small and medium-sized firms should be
improved by:

(a) developing and coordinating vocational training,
     retraining, and technical assistance;

(b) improving the financial machinery to allow small and medium-sized firms easier access to risk capital and credit without curtailing their independence *vis-à-vis* large firms;

(c) favouring the creation and establishment of new enterprises capable of innovating and responding to the needs of society, and in particular *cooperative* enterprise owned and controlled by the workforce itself.

(d) ensuring that all small and medium-sized firms have access to technological developments through joint research centres and, in the same field, reviewing the rules on the period of validity of patents and licences;

(e) making it compulsory for public purchasing to be subcontracted through to the level of small and medium-sized firms.

The new economic strategy proposed does not necessarily mean systematic surveillance of all prices. Instead, the prices of meso-economic firms, and those firms occupying a dominant position on a specific market could be monitored and made subject to social control. This applies particularly to firms working on public contracts.

Prices policy should also be strengthened by:

(a) requiring manufacturers (and importers) to give prior notification of increases in the prices of certain key products (prices with a high inflationary potential);

(b) obliging exclusive distributors to make available their price lists and other conditions of sale for inclusion in a public register. Participation in an unauthorized restrictive price agreement should also be classified and penalized as an offence.

It is often not within the power of a single member state to ensure effective surveillance of the price policy of meso-economic multinational firms. The information neeeded to coordinate surveillance of the prices practised by these firms should therefore be collected at Community level with a view to detecting and combating compensatory dumping, transfer-pricing (and thus profit transfer) within a meso-economic firm, i.e., fixing different levels of prices or profit margins for a number of products in the same country, for the same product in various countries or for a number of products in various countries. Such information collated at the Community level could vastly reinforce the effective intervention of respective nation states in the Community.

To make the cost levels and structures, prices and profit margins of meso-economic firms comparable, an *accounting plan for firms* could be made compulsory for meso-economic enterprise and a simplified version could be introduced for other firms. This plan should set down minimum guidelines for the presentation of firms' accounts and the rules for entering transactions and stocks in the accounts (evaluation, definition of periods, etc.) and for the calculation of significant ratios (profitability, etc.)

For the purpose of monitoring transfer-pricing, export and import transactions between national subsidiaries of multinational firms should be presented in separate disaggregated form in international trade statistics.

Clearly, all the changes proposed in the preceding chapters will not come about spontaneously.

Hence the *vital importance of planning*, not merely as a forecasting instrument for analysing future possibilities and risks, but as an effective instrument for guiding the economy in new directions granted the highly varied choice of possible means of action. Such planning should be focused on both public enterprise and public accountability in the meso-economic sector, and a combination of both public assistance and new modes of ownership and control in the micro-economic sector (e.g., cooperative enterprise and enterprise under direct workers' control).

If it is to be effective, planning must fulfil certain *fundamental conditions*. Planning must be an instrument which is democratic in its formulation; rigorously coherent and strict in its strategic priorities once established; and adjustable from year to year, while maintaining medium- and long-term perspectives. But it also must be made more rigorous by the use of an integrated data processing system using detailed socio-economic accounts.

Planning prepared on the basis of alternative strategies, and culminating in a schedule of precise objectives, must be the main instrument in the dialogue between public authorities and the two sides of industry, trade unions and management (whether conventional or worker controlled). It should include other activities aimed particularly at linking part of the short-term budget more closely to the medium- and long-term plan; carrying out the structural adjustments required both by international constraints and by the introduction of the new development model; and ensuring effective surveillance and monitoring of meso-economic firms.

The integrated data-processing system is an essential prerequisite for more effective and constructive social negotiation in a planning framework. It must serve in each country as a basis for a *socio-economic model* on which alternative courses of action and strategies set out in reference tables can be established, showing the weight given to particular specific objectives and the means needed to implement them.

Preparation and discussion of alternative or optional schedules should culminate in a target table containing overall guidelines and norms concerning:

(a) allocation of the national product by economic sector and function, plus the regional distribution of the means of production;
(b) public expenditure and income;
(c) the structure of economic finance, notably investment;
(d) money and credit;
(e) personal incomes (earned and unearned) and social incomes;
(f) the qualitative benefits from development, in terms of the new social indicators.

If it is to cover the various types of objectives and actions adequately, planning must not only be three-dimensional by incorporating structural, social, and spatial distribution, but must include a *long-term* plan (15–20 years) as the strategy for changing the mode of development. Objectives which can be attained only after a fairly long period should be fixed: the structure of national consumption, wealth and the labour market, the education system, regional planning, etc. Long-term plans should be divided into sub-periods laying down medium-term policy objectives. Planning must also represent a rolling *medium-term* plan (5 years) with particular emphasis on priority investment programmes, disaggregated annually with intermediate objectives.

It is in this framework that the links between national budgets (annual sections of the plans) and the medium-term plans themselves should be stengthened, and above all, that the link between the state budget (including social security) and the plan should be reinforced.

Principles and Procedures

Although technically equipped to make a coherent choice between the objectives of society and the means of attaining them and thus strike a lasting blow against inflation, the main protagonists on the economic and social scene must respect a number of essential principles:

(a) enlarging the scope of involvement in planning negotiation, on the basis of the new enlarged social and economic accounting already proposed;

(b) tri-partite bargaining of change in the meso-economic sector, on the lines of Planning Agreements between government, trade unions and management;

(c) coherent involvement, on the basis of information and negotiation, of regional and local representatives institutions;

(d) a central body for the coordination of planning procedures, within the heart of government (either a department or preferably a Cabinet Committee for Economic Planning in which spending ministers could countervail the shorter-term and defensive postures of finance ministers);

(e) parliamentary powers for extensive evaluation, criticism and challenge to the planning process as evolved at other levels, including both sub-committees with real investigative and scrutiny capacity, and full parliamentary debate and decision-making.

Coherent and democratic planning based on an exhaustive analysis of requirements must define the priorities adopted more clearly than has been done in the past. In the present circumstances, the emphasis must be on planning increased public expenditure and production by public enterprise without endangering the balance of public finance and restimulating inflation, substantially through a better match of effective taxation and public spending, and organizing the redeployment of investment, production, employment and incomes.

The national plans must contain an obligatory section *covering priority public expenditure* for the planned development strategy. This obligatory section would take the following form: An overall ceiling and individual ceilings would be fixed for the major categories. Major programmes would be defined within each of these ceilings (covering both operating expenditure and capital expenditure), and the necessary cyclical flexibility for implementing the annual budget would therefore be maintained within the ceilings fixed.

The redeployment of investment and production must be planned at national level in such a manner that public purchasing becomes focused on those firms which agree to be contractually bound to the planned redeployment organized by the public authorities and especially on that meso-economic enterprise which registers a major impact on macro-economic aggregates. The instruments for such a policy – but with the crucial additional inclusion of trade union representatives – already exist in several countries (Planning Agreements, *contrats de programme*, *contrats de progrès*, *contrattazione programmatica*, etc.). To have a reasonable chance of success, this policy must be negotiated with trade union representatives in individual agreements of the Planning Agreements type in the meso-economic sector. The new planning must focus at the same time on both economic objectives and the new social ends, notably on promotion of means for adaptation and conversion of activities, the new employment criteria, new training for

workers in guaranteed jobs, the social redistribution of
employment and income.

Ideologically, such perspectives represent a transformation of
the kind of planning ends and means which became part of the
conventional wisdom in the postwar period. They represent a
challenge to the power of private capital in key sectors of the
modern economy to determine what should be produced, why,
where, how and for whom, without countervailance by the
public authorities, trade unions, and other interested parties.

Nevertheless, irrespective of the specific form of crisis in the
economy following the recession of the 1970s, such new
dimensions to the social and political negotiation of change
have been brought on to the agenda of contemporary European
economies by the crisis of the postwar mode of development
itself.

If governments and management hesitate to implement the
extension of democratic procedures implicit in the proposed
new mode of development, they should not be surprised by a
different challenge to the principles of democracy, of a kind
which could represent a historic reversal of democratic
government itself.

Contributors

FRANCO ARCHIBUGI Professor of Planning at the University of Calabria and Director of the Centre for Economic Planning Studies, Rome. Formerly a Director General in the European Coal and Steel Community and Senior Consultant to the Ministry of the Budget and Economic Programming. Author of various articles and contributions to symposia. Also editor of several volumes on economic planning published by the Centre for Economic Planning Studies.

JACQUES ATTALI Auditeur au Conseil d'Etat, Maître de Conferences a l'École Polytechnique, Professor of Economics at the University of Paris IX and Economic Adviser to François Mitterand. Author of *L'Anti-Economique* (with Marc Guillaume) 1974, *La Parole et l'Outil* 1975, and *Bruits* 1976.

THOMAS BALOGH Formerly Fellow of Balliol College Oxford, Special Economic Adviser to the Prime Minister 1964–7, and thereafter Special Consultant. Life peer 1970. Minister of State, Department of Energy 1974–6. Vice-Chairman British National Oil Corporation 1976–8. Consultant to various governments, including Malta, Jamaica, Greece. Many publications, including *Planning for Progress* 1963, *Economics of Poverty* 1966, etc.

JACQUES DELORS Formerly responsible for Social Affairs at the Commissariat du Plan and Special Adviser on Social Affairs to Jacques Chaban-Delmas when he was Prime Minister. Responsible for main elements of social reform programme of French government 1969–72. Social Affairs adviser to François Mitterand and the French Socialist Party. Currently Professor at the University of Paris IX and Director of the Work and Society Research Institute. Author of *Les Indicateurs Sociaux* 1971 and *Changer* (with Claude Glayman) 1971.

STUART HOLLAND Formerly Economic Assistant Cabinet Office and Personal Assistant to the Prime Minister 1966–8. Subsequently Research Fellow and Lecturer in European Studies, Sussex University. Special Adviser to Commons Expenditure Committee, 1971–2, to Minister of Overseas Development 1974–5, etc. Author (*inter alia*) of *The Socialist Challenge* 1975, *The Regional Problem* 1976.

GIORGIO RUFFOLO Formerly Director General of Economic Planning in the Ministry of the Budget and Economic Programming, Rome. Responsible for introduction of *Contrattazione programmatica* (Italian version of Planning Agreements). Author of *Riforme e Controriforme* 1974 and (with others) of *Progetto Socialista* 1976.

NORBERT WIECZOREK Formerly Assistant Professor of Economics at the Technical University of Aachen. Currently economist with the Cooperative Bank (Bank für Gemeinwirtschaft), Frankfurt. Responsible with Karl Georg Zinn and Werner Meissner for formulation of SPD proposals on *Investitionslenkung* and *Strukturpolitik*.

KARL GEORG ZINN Professor of Economics at the Technical University of Aachen. Co-author with Norbert Wieczorek and Werner Meissner of new planning policies accepted by the SPD in 1975 (see above). Author (*inter alia*) of *Strategien gegen di Arbeitslosigkeit* 1977 and of further books on Economic Planning, the Labour Theory of Value, etc.

References

Chapter 1   The Decline of French Planning

1. A point stressed by Andrew Shonfield in his *Modern Capitalism*, OUP–RIIA, 1965.
2. See further Shonfield's extensive argument, *ibid.*, Chapter 5, *The Etatist Tradition: France*.
3. See Pierre Massé, *Le Plan ou l'Anti-Hasard*, Gallimard, 1965.
4. *Inter alia* on the Medium Term Economic Policy Committee of the EEC, set up by Robert Marjolin in 1964. Marjolin had been involved at a senior level with the First French Plan, and tried via this EEC Committee to establish medium-term planning within the Community framework.
5. The French Communist Party's conception of planning in France as serving the interests of monopoly capital was developed in the early 1960s and has been most extensively expressed in the PCF symposium of Paul Boccara, Jeanne-Marie Bourdet, and others, *Le Capitalisme Monopoliste d'Etat*, Editions Sociales, 2 vols., 1971.
6. The non-cooperation of the automobile manufacturers was notorious. The planners were forced to resort to estimating the trend in global production from available figures on vehicle registrations.
7. Trade union representation on the Modernization Commissions of successive plans was low – never more than 16 per cent of the total from the First to Fifth plans, but fell to less than six per cent on the Second Plan and was less than eight per cent on the Third. It rose to 21 per cent on the Sixth Plan. See Pierre Pascallon, *La planification de l'économie française*, Table 15, Masson et Cie, 1974.
8. For two further analyses of the extent to which EEC entry and increased liberalization of market forces undermined French planning during this period see Jean Bénard, *L'avenir de la planification française*, Revue Économique, 1964, and Bela Balassa, *Whither French Planning?*, Quarterly Journal of Economics, 1965.
9. This two-sidedness of public and social expenditure, as providing

demand for output from privately owned productive enterprise, and improving the quality of public services which they use, is stunningly overlooked in the simplist monetarist case for public expenditure cuts. (Ed.)

10. The percentage shortfall on individual projects, of which much has been made by Vera Lutz in her book *Central Planning for the Market Economy* (Longmans, 1969), was less important than the fact that the Plan managed to promote an overall shift in resources and expenditure. Mrs. Lutz largely misses the wood for the trees.

11. This should be even though the methods of realization are not the same in both cases.

Chapter 2   Towards Socialist Planning

1. For an elaboration of these concepts see further Jacques Attali, *La Parole et l'Outil*, Chapters 4 and 5, Presses Universitaires de France, 1975.

2. *Ibid.*, pp. 89–98.

3. *Ibid.*, pp. 121–2.

4. See further, *ibid.*, Chapters 6 and 13, and Jacques Attali, *Bruits*, Presses Universitaires de France, 1977.

Chapter 3   Capitalist Planning in Question

1. See, *inter alia*, Pasquale Saraceno, *Ricostruzione e Pianificazione 1943–1948*, Laterza, 1969.

2. Ministero del Bilancio e della Programmazione Economica, *Schema di Sviluppo dell'occupazione e del Reddito in Italia nel Decennto 1955–64*, December 1955.

3. *Dibittato alla Camera dei Deputati sulla politica Meridionalistica*, in *Informazioni Svimez*, No. 6, 1961.

4. See Chapter 7 (Ed.).

5. Ministero del Bilancio e della Programmazione Economica, *Progretto di Programma di Sviluppo Economico per il Quinquennio 1966–70*, January 1965.

6. On the experience of *contrattazione programmatica*, see further Giorgio Ruffolo, Rapporto sulla *Programmazione*, Ministero del Bilancio e della Programmazione Economica, 1973, and S. Petriccione, *Politica Industriale e Mezzogiorno*, Laterza, 1976.

7. Ministero del Bilancio e della Programmazione Econmica, Progetto '80 – *Rapporto Preliminare al Programma Economico Nazionale 1971–75*, 2 vols. April 1969.

8. Ministero del Bilancio e della Programmazione Economica. *Programma Economico Nazionale 1971–75*, 1972.
9. For an elaboration of this argument see further Franco Archibugi, *A Progress Report: The Quality of Life in a Method of Integrated Planning*, in *Socio-Economic Planning Sciences*, Vol. 8, 1975.

Chapter 4 Project for Socialist Planning

1. This chapter is derived from Giorgio Ruffolo and others, *Progetto Socialista*, 1976, pp. 3–54. The editor gratefully acknowledges the permission of Laterza & Figli Spa Rome–Bari for the extracts.
2. Ernest Mandel, *Late Capitalism*, New Left Books, 1975. (First published as *Der Spätkapitalismus*, Suhrkamp Verlag, 1972.)

Chapter 5 The 'Social Market' in Crisis

1. A brief sketch of postwar German economic development is given by K. Hardach, *Germany 1914–1970*, in M. Cipolla, ed., *The Fontana Economic History of Europe*, Vol. 6, Collins/Fontana, 1976.
2. Since the beginning of the 1970s there has been a clear shift from investment for new capacity to more rationalization. Of course investment in previous years had always partly included rationalization, but this was generally combined with the widening of productive capacity. But since 1970–71 the share of rationalization to total investment has been rising steeply. The investment polls of the Münich Ifo-Institute, which are comparable to the polls of the Confederation of British Industry, show that the motive to rationalize' is dominant, outstripping replacement and new capacity. This trend was not curbed by the 'profit-explosion' of 1976, when the rate of profit increase exceeded 26 per cent. On the contrary, the investment poll for autumn 1976 showed that about 87 per cent of the firms interviewed by Ifo-Institute intended to invest in order to rationalize over the medium-term (until 1980). Only 10 per cent of enterprise is planning capacity growth. This should not be surprising since excess capacity amounted to some 25 per cent in 1975. Thus growing profits are no guarantee for growing investment and/or creation of new jobs; profits might be a favourable condition for investment but the necessary condition is a growth of demand.
3. The high saving rate is partly due to the migrant labourers, who show an extremely high propensity to save because of intended

establishment of a self-employed existence in their home countries later on and/or because of the transfer payments to their families. It is evident that the saving behaviour of migrant labourers had been an advantage to the stabilization of the cost-of-living price index especially. Thus the migrant labourers helped to keep down the wage-rates and the consumption price level.

4. *Cf.* Walter Eucken, *Grundsätze der Wirtschaftspolitik*, 2nd ed., Tübingen-Zürich, 1955.

5. *Cost of living index for the Federal Republic 1970=100*

1962	1963	1964	1965	1966	1967	1968
81·6	84·0	85·9	88·7	91·9	93·4	94·9

1969	1970	1971	1972	1973	1974	1975
96·7	100	105·3	111·1	118·8	127·1	134·7

Source: *Monatsberichte der Deutschen Bundesbank*, May 1976, p. 68.

6. *Balance of current account for the Federal Republic (Billion Deutschmarks)*

1960	1961	1962	1963	1964	1965	1966	1967
+4·78	+3·19	−1·58	+0·99	+0·52	−6·22	+0·48	+10·00

1968	1969	1970	1971	1972	1973	1974	1975
+11·85	+7·49	+3·18	+3·08	+2·47	+11·49	+25·13	+9·19

Source: *Monatsberichte der Deutschen Bundesbank*, May 1976, p. 70.

7. *Five-year average of comparable wage ratios in the Federal Republic (Wages to National Income)*

1950/4	1955/9	1960/4	1965/9	1970/4
56·5	54·5	54·8	54·5	56·5

See W. Glastetter, *Die wirtschaftliche Entwicklung in der Bundesrepublik Deutschland im Zeitraum 1970 bis 1975. Ein empirischer Befund*, in: Industriegewerkschaft Metall, ed., *Materialien zur*

Tagung Krise und Reform in der Industriesgesellschaft, Frankfurt/M 1976, p. 59.

8. *Five-year average growth rates of GNP in the Federal Republic*

1950/4	1955/9	1960/4	1965/9	1970/4
8·7	6·7	5·3	4·2	3·6

Source: Glastetter, *Die wirtschaftliche Entwicklung* . . . , p. 59.

9. *Gesetz zur Förderung der Stabilität und des Wachstums der Wirtschaft,* 8th June, 1967.
10. *Cf.* the figures for 1967 to 1969, footnote 6.
11. *Cf.* note 5.
12. See Stuart Holland, *Meso-Economics, New Public Enterprise and Democratic Planning,* Annals of Public and Cooperative Economy, April–June 1974, and *The Socialist Challenge,* 1975.
13. For concentration figures, see *Bericht des Bundeskartellamtes über seine Tätigkeit im Jahre 1975,* Bundestagsdrucksache; *Gutachten der Monopolkommission 1976* (§ 24b *Gesetz gegen Wettbewerbsbeschränkungen*); Arndt Ed., Helmut, *Die Konzentration in der Wirtschaft,* 2 vols., Schriften des Vereins für Socialpolitik, vols. 20/I, 20/II, Berlin–München, 1971.
14. The following authors give an impression of the recent discussion about the problem of 'Investitionslenkung'. T. Sarrazin, ed., *Investitionslenkung,* Bonn-Bad Godesberg, 1976; G. Fleischele/M. Krüper, eds., *Investitionslenkung. Überwindung oder Ergänzung der Marktwirtschaft?,* Frankfurt/M – Köln, 1975; ZH. Besters, ed., *Investitionslenkung – Bedrohung der Marktwirtschaft?,* Köln, 1976; W. Roth, ed., *Investitionslenkung,* Reinbek, 1976; Werner Meissner, *Investitionslenkung,* Frankfurt/M, 1974; W. Meissner, N. Wieczorek, K. G. Zinn, *Veränderung der Machtverhältnisse und Verbesserung der Lebensqualität. Überlegungen zum ökonomisch-politischen Oreintierungsrahmen,* in: *Die Neue Gesellschaft,* Vol. 20/1, January 1973, p. 56 ff. – (this was the first article about 'Investitionslenkung' during the recent discussion).
15. It is important to stress that the need to revise the constitution of the Federal Republic played a key role in the decision that the plan would not be directly compulsory for private companies.
16. The idea of controlling private investment finds some friends among those economists who are representing the interests of big business and are pleading for investment-cartels. *Cf.* A. Sölter,

Investitionswettbewerb und Investitionskontrolle, Köln, 1973.
17. For a brief sketch of the several 'schools' of 'Investionslenkung' *cf.* K. G. Zinn, *Investitionskontrolle*, in *Wörterbuch zur politischen Ökonomie*, 2nd ed., Opladen 1977.

Chapter 6   Perspectives for Planning

1. Vorstand der SPD, *Grundsatz Programm der Sozialdemokratischen Partei Deutschlands* (Bad Godesberg, 13–15 November 1959) Druckhaus Deutz, Cologne.
2. Vorstand der SPD, *Ökonomisch-politicher Orientierungsrahm für die Jahre 1975–85*, Mannheim, 14 November 1975. English translation, *Framework of Economic and Political Orientation of the Social Democratic Party of Germany for the Years 1975–6*, Kölner Strasse 149, D-5300, Bonn Bad-Godesberg, 1976.
3. In 1977, the DGB produced several critiques of the crisis of employment, including (a) *Stellungsnahme des DGB zur Beschäftigungspolitik*, and (b) *Vorschläge des DGB zur Wiederherstellung der Vollbeschäftigung*, reprinted in Karl Georg Zinn (ed.) *Strategien gegen die Arbeitslosigkeit*, Section IV (Documents), Europäische Verlaganstalt, 1977.

Chapter 7   Britain's Planning Problems

1. See in particular the case as argued by Friedrich Von Hayek, *The Road to Serfdom*, Routledge, 1944.
2. Partly because of the complications of Suez.
3. *Cf.* Jack Downie, *The Competitive Process*, Duckworth, 1957.
4. See further, Thomas Balogh, *Planning for Progress*, Fabian Society, 1963. This paper was frankly against devaluation unless there were reserves of idle resources and a firm 'social contract' with the unions. This we could not have in the autumn of 1964, when the Maudling boom was at its height and the unions full of suspicions. All economic advisers – as is well known – advocated devaluation in 1966, and I was, in addition, in favour of the strictest tightening of exchange control. It was implemented – as usual too little, too late – at great cost in lost national income and unemployment.
5. I introduced George Brown to MacDougall, MacIntosh, and other economists whom I thought highly of, and they played an important role in the Department.
6. F. H. Hahn, *On the Notion of Equilibrium in Economics*, CUP, London, 1973.

Chapter 8   Planning Disagreements

1. See, *inter alia*, Wilfred Beckerman and Andrew Graham, in Wilfred Beckerman (ed.) *The Labour Government's Economic Record*, Duckworth, Chapter 1.

2. Anthony Crosland, *The Future of Socialism*, Jonathan Cape (paperback revised edition), 1964.

3. Various partial prototypes of Planning Agreement were devised by Robert Maldague, Head of the Belgian Plan, in the late 1960s and made available in essence by him to the author in the background research leading to the formulation of Planning Agreements in Labour Party policy. They included *contrats de programme*, which focused mainly on price behaviour and agreements in big business; *contrats de progrès*, concerned with major innovations and productivity advances; *contrats de gestion*, involving management changes in business as a condition for government contracts and *contrats prototype*, specifying agreement on terms for public sponsorship of private research and development.

   The French *contrats de programme* introduced in 1968 were nominally about prices, but in practice concerned an attempt to evaluate the cost structures on which big business submitted the case for price increases, including not only the contribution of R and D, but also import prices in trade from subsidiaries abroad, component and labour costs etc.

4. The Labour Party, Opposition Green Paper, *The National Enterprise Board*, July 1973.

5. The Labour Party, *Labour's Programme*, 1973, pp. 17–18.

6. HMSO, *In Place of Strife*, Cmnd. 3888, London, 1968.

7. *Cf.* S. J. Prais, who elaborates an analysis of the share of the top 100 manufacturing companies in *The Evolution of Giant Firms in Britain*, Cambridge University Press and the National Institute of Economic and Social Research, 1976.

8. Department of Trade, *Direct Exporters and the Credit Terms of Exports, Trade and Industry*, April 1974, and Monopolies Commission, *A Survey of Mergers*, 1970.

9. United Nations, *Multinational Corporations in World Development*, New York, 1973.

10. British Export Trade Research Organisation, *Concentration on Key Markets*, April 1975.

11. See *inter alia* the evidence of the Financial Director of Burroughs in House of Commons, 2nd Report from the Expenditure

Committee, *Regional Development Incentives*, Minutes of Evidence, 1974.

12. *Investment in Britain A Survey, The Economist*, 12 November 1977.

13. The 'gelding' of the obligatory powers of *Labour's Programme* 1973 and the February 1974 Manifesto had already occurred by the time of the appearance of the euphemistically mis-titled White Paper, *The Regeneration of British Industry*, Cmnd 5710, August 1974.

14. Roy Jenkins, in *What Matters Now*, Collins–Fontana, 1972, Chapter 2 (*The Needs of the Regions*) argues the case for a major State Holding Company similar in essentials to the National Enterprise Board, on the basis that regional incentives no longer bite effectively on big business. He appears to have neglected or contradicted this argument by his present endorsement of an allegedly efficacious European Regional Fund, much as he condemned in 1973 the Labour Party's proposals for a major State Holding Company, which in practice were virtually identical with his own.

15. Robert Bacon and Walter Eltis, *Britain's Economic Problem: Too Few Producers*, Macmillan 1976 (2nd edition 1978).

16. Under prevailing circumstances in Britain it appears that one has to be either a retired Permanent Under-Secretary or a deceased Cabinet Minister to be able to breach the Official Secrets Act with impunity. Certainly Richard Crossman's *Diaries of a Cabinet Minister*, Jonathan Cape and Hamish Hamilton, 1975–77, are an encyclopaedia of information on oligarchic dominance of officialdom in government. Implicitly, they reveal the extent to which civil servants, thinking themselves neutral, nevertheless think within the parameters either of the prevailing liberal capitalist ideology or that ideology which they imbued with Oxbridge in their late and impressionable adolescence.

17. In Britain the case has been organized by the Campaign for Labour Party Democracy, and reflected in the argument for automatic re-selection of Labour members of Parliament (paralleling the automatic re-selection of Labour Councillors). See also the excellent analysis of Ken Coates, *Democracy in the Labour Party*, Spokesman Books, 1977.

18. Jürgen Habermas, *Legitimation Crisis*, Heinemann, 1976.

19. For an analysis of the differences between consensus building for social democratic management of capitalism, and the more Gramscian consensus building of the PCI see further Stuart Holland, *The New Communist Economics*, in Edward Mortimer,

Paolo Filo della Toree and Jonathan Story (eds.) *Eurocommunism*, Penguin Books and Mondadori, 1978.

Chapter 9   The International Crisis

1. See further EEC Commission, *Sixth Report on Competition Policy*, 1976, and L. G. Franko, *The European Multinationals*, Harper and Row, 1976.
2. See further EEC Commission, *Fifth Report on Competition Policy*, 1975 (Introduction and summary of the research programme on concentration).
3. For the 'price umbrella' concept see Edith Penrose, *The Theory of the Growth of the Firm*, Basil Blackwell, 1959.
4. Such a situation relates very much to what the late Professor Fred Hirsch called 'positional goods', in *The Social Limits to Growth*, Routledge, 1977.
5. In 1970, the figure for Germany was 41 per cent, for the Netherlands 51 per cent, and the United Kingdom 58 per cent.
6. In Italy, the percentage was 109 per cent.
7. Traditional private consumption plus goods and services provided free of charge to households by the public authorities.
8. *Expenditure Trends in OECD Countries, 1960–1980*; OECD, July 1972.
9. 'Pure' private consumption is defined as follows by OECD: 'Consumption not paid for out of transfers received from the public sector in connection with social security and other welfare schemes.' *ibid.*, p. 11.
10. The national accounts of the member countries that have adopted the new conventions of the European System of Integrated Economic Accounts (ESA) contain two distinct and uncoordinated functional classifications based on the United Nations' System of National Accounts (1970):

   one showing general government expenditure (see Table 12 of the SOEC National Accounts Yearbook 1973) (breakdown to one digit of the United Nations classification);
   the other showing final consumption of households (see Table 7 of the SOEC National Accounts Yearbook 1973).

   Apart from the national accounts, work on functional breakdowns has been carried out or is still going on in two other fields:

   social accounts: a functional breakdown of social security expenditure (*cf.* SOEC publications);

public finance: a functional breakdown of public expenditure beyond the second digit of the United Nations classification (*cf.* OECD works).

In September 1973 OECD attempted, unsuccessfully, to establish a combined functional classification of public and private expenditure.

11. See further EEC Commission, *European Regional Development Fund*, (First Annual Report), 1976, which admitted that GDP per head increased from five to one to six to one in favour of Hamburg and against South Italy between 1970 and 1975.

Chapter 10   Planning for Development

1. See further, *Second Report from the Expenditure Committee, Regional Development Incentives*, Minutes of Evidence, 1974.

Index

References in **bold characters** denote chapters or sections that are wholly concerned with the subjects to which they refer.

Advertising, 78, 171, 172, 176, 188
allocation of resources *see* resource allocation and distribution
anti-inflationary policy, 87–9, 92, 95, 101, 165

Balance of payments, 17, 21, 85, 91, 96, 123, 125–6, 128, 130, 149, 154, 182
balance of trade *see* trade
big business *see* meso-economic sector, monopoloy, multi-national companies
BNOC (British National Oil Corporation), 135–6
borrowing, 132, 143, 188
Britain, **121–61**; postwar planning, 121–32, NEDC, 123–6, National Plan, 126–9; public ownership and planning, 133–6; Labour Party and planning role, 137–8; meso-economic sector, 139–42; new planning strategy and failure of implementation, 138–59 *passim*
British Leyland, 134, 152

British National Oil Corporation *see* BNOC
British Petroleum, 135
Bundesbank see *Deutsche Bundesbank*

Capital accumulation, 86, 88–91, 95; rate of German capital growth, *table* 91
capitalist crisis, 1–2, 34–7, 61, 69–74, 85, 98, 142–4, 153–4, 158–60, 165–8, 184
capitalist planning, **1–4**; Britain, 121–30; France, 9–29; Germany, 99–103, 106–9; Italy, 49–53, 56–61 *passim*; challenge to capitalist planning from European Left, 2–6 *passim*, 16, 34–40, 62, 79–80, 117, 156–61
cartelization, 93, 133, 209 *note* 16
Central Planning Council (France), 26
Christian Democrat Party (Germany), 98, 106–7, 110, 114
Christian Democrat Party (Italy), 50
Civil Service (UK), 121, 123–4, 126, 130, 136, 155, 156

Commissariat du Plan, 9, 16, 21, 25–6
commodity prices, 132, 143, 154, 166
Common Programme of the French Left, 2, 4, 37–46
communications, 44, 74, 76; see also information
Communist Party: France, 38, 205 note 5; Germany, 108; Italy, 159–60
competition policies, 22, 92–3, 100, 101, 103–4, 108, 110, 112, 114, 137, 170; see also demand management, market mechanism
concentration of capital, 35–6, 72, 93, 97, 101, 103, 139–41; see also meso-economic sector, monopoly, multinational companies
Conservative Party (UK): in government, 122–3, 125–6, 129–30; industrial relations legislation, 145, 151
consumption and demand, domestic, 18, 19, 38–9, 86–91 passim, 101, 123, 125–6, 130, 143, 175–6, 179, 184, 188
contrattazione programmatica, 51–3, 138
cultural activities, 19, chart 66–7, 176, 189–90

DDR see German Democratic Republic
DEA (Department of Economic Affairs), 127–9
decentralization of planning, 39–46, 74–9, 180–2
deflation, 5, 85, 87, 129, 137, 158, 175, 182

demand see consumption and demand, domestic
demand management, 88, 97–100, 103–4, 109–10, 141, 166–7; see also competition policies, market mechanism
democracy and planning, 6, 16, 29–33, 40–6, 74–9, 156–61 passim, 192–5, 198; see also industrial democracy; negotiation, social; social democracy
Department of Economic Affairs see DEA
Deutsche Bundesbank, 86–7, 99
Deutschmark: revaluation, 91, 92, 94, table 95, 98; undervaluation, 86, 88, 91, 95, 97
devaluation of sterling, 121, 125–6, 128–9, 137, 141, 210 note 4
development: implosive, 41–4; new model of development, 184–92, 199–202; see also growth
distribution of resources see resource allocation and distribution

Economists and planning, 124, 127–8
education, 19, 27, 28, 30, 43, chart 66, 80, 90, 188
EEC, 5–6, 18, 131, 148, 169, 180; and inflation, 166, 175; intervention/response at Community level, 62, 117, 167, 185, 196–8, 205 note 4; movement of workers and structural unemployment, 167, 172–4
emigrant labour, 87–8, 95
employment policies, 3, 22, 173–4, 190; full employment,

employment policies—*cont.*
3, 35–6, 38, 71, 96–8, 127, 130,
149, 166, 173–4, 187; *see also*
unemployment
ENI (National Hydrocarbons
Corporation), 52, 136
environment, 19, 30, *chart* 67, 73,
187
Eucken, Walter, 'Foundations of
Economic Policy', 97, 108
European Economic Community
see EEC
European Left and the challenge
to capitalist planning, 2–6
passim, 16, 34–40, 62, 79–80,
117, 156–61; *see also* socialist
planning
exchange rates, 87, 92, 94–5, 131,
140, 182, 210 *note* 4
exchange value, 42, 56–7
exports, 187; British, 121–3, 132,
140–3, 149, 169; German, 85,
87–8, 90–2, 93–7, 101, 106

Fifth French Plan, 20–3
First French Plan, 12–17
first Italian five-year plan *see*
Pieraccini Plan
fiscal policy as planning
instrument, 14–15, 18, 70,
87–8, 99, 101, 128, 141, 182,
190
forecasting, 9–11, 15, 26–7; *see
also* social accounting, social
indicators
*Four Year Plan, The (New
Statesman)*, quoted 127
Fourth French Plan, 20
France, 9–46, 125–6, 129, 131;
characteristics of society, 9–10;
goals of planning, 10–12; key
periods for planning, 12–13;

Plans, 12–23; bipolarization of
politics and refusal to plan,
23–9 *passim*; democratic planning, 29–33; capitalist crisis,
35–6; Common Programme of
the French Left, 37–46
Friedman, Milton, 1, 158

German Democratic Republic,
88, 89, 105, 106–7
Germany, Federal Republic of,
85–117; post-war economic
development and recent
decline, 85–90; as exporting
country, 92–7; social market
philosophy and government
economic policy, 97–108;
Godesberg Programme,
108–9; investment control
and *Orientierungsrahm*, 104–5,
110–17
Giscard d'Estaing, President V.,
20, 24, 26–7; 'Giscard
dirigism', 9, 27
GNP, 42, 56, 132, *table* 209 *note* 8
Godesberg Programme (1959),
108–9, 112, 114–15
growth, economic, 179, 184, 189;
French, 11–12, 13–17, 18, 24,
36, 40, explosive, 42–5, 49;
German, 85–93, 93–5, 102,
106, rate of German capital
growth, *table* 91, growth rates
of German GNP, *table* 209 *note*
8; Italian, 49, 56, 71, 72–3; *see
also* development

Health, 19, 27, 28, *table* 66, 80,
188
Heath, Edward, 129–30, 146, 151
housing, 17, 27, *chart* 67–8, 176,
189

IMF (International Monetary Fund), 148, 154
immigrant labour, 72, 88–9, 95, 98
imperative planning *see* nationalization, public enterprise
imports, 45, 122; prices, 132, 143, 154, 172, 187
incomes: distribution, 3, 30, 44, *chart* 66, 177, 185; inequality, 36, 107, 165, 180, 184; levels, 70–2 *passim*, 86, 98, 100–1, 109, 130, 171, 177, *table* 208 *note* 7; redistribution, 14, 20, 23, 24, 38, 55, 75–6, 98, 190–1; *see also* social security transfers *under* social security
incomes policies, 21–4, 76, 92, 98–101, 128–30, 139, 143–6, 151, 154, 157–8, 175; social contract, 145–6; 'stop-go' policies, 123, 125, 129, 167–8, 175
indicative planning, 1, 34, 125, 131, 139, 140, 147, 157
industrial democracy, 3–6, 29–31, 38–40, 111, 155–9; *see also* democracy and planning; negotiation, social; social democracy
industrial relations, 128, 145–6, 180; *see also* negotiation, social
Industrial Relations Act, 130
Industrial Reorganization Committee, 147
Industry Act (1975), 146
inequality, 31, 45, 55, 75–6, 107; *see also* inequality *under* incomes
inflation: Britain, 128–30, 140–3, 154; France, 10, 18, 20–4 *passim*, 36, 42, 45; Germany, 87–8, 91, 95, 98–101 *passim*;

Italy, 70, 72, 76; international, 1, 5, 94–6, 131, **165–8**, 172, 175–83; inflationary price behaviour in meso-economic sector, 140–1, 154, 175, 182; action against inflation, 184–5
information, 10–11, 43–6, 73–8, 193–6
intervention, state *see* state intervention
Investitionskontrolle, 104–5
Investitionslenkung, 104–5, 115
investment, 1, 14–18, 35, 44, 90, 122, 140–3, 165, 167; grants and subsidies, 14–15, 18, 27, 51, 86, 89, 99, 104, 113, 145, 177, 192, 195; state control/intervention, 18, 39, 99, 102–5, 108, 110–16, 126–30, 133–4, 145, 188–90, *contrattazione programmatica*, 51–3
Italy, **49–81**; history of planning, 49–50; regional investment, 51–3; *Progetto Ottanta* and longer-term planning, 53–5; new methodology for planning, 55–68; capitalist and political crisis, 69–74; democratic decentralized planning, 74–9; strategy for transition to socialism, **79–81**

Keynesian economics, 1, 71, 88, **99–101**, 103, 109, 125, 126, 139, 140, 148, 154, 158, 166–7; *see also* competition policies, demand management, market mechanism

Labour Party (UK): in government, 122, 126–9, 130,

Labour Party (UK)—*cont.*
142; and oil sector, 135; new planning strategy and failure of implementation, 137–59 *passim*
labour supply, 29–31, 71–2, 86–91 *passim*, 95, 98, 142, 149, 172–4; turnover, 24, 177; *see also* employment policies, unemployment

Macro-economics: theory, 103, 140, 168; policies, 18, 20, 22, 137
Maldague Report (1976), 5–6
Mannheim Programme (1975), 4, 114–15
manufacturing industry, 51–3, 125, 133, 139–40, 148–9, 192
'market conformism' philosophy, 97
market mechanism, 2, 10–11, 17, 18–19, 39, 96, 133–4; liberalization, 22, 78, 123, 131; and planning, 32, 56–7; *see also* competition policies, demand management, social market philosophy
meso-economic sector, 23, 73, 166–7, 168–72, 174–5, 184; theory, 102–3, 168; investment, 18, 28, 51–2, 102–3, 111–13, 191–2; and planning, 13, 32, 111–13, 117, 139–50 *passim*, 185, 189, 193–202 *passim*; price-making power, 70, 140–2, 169–72, 174–5; relationship with the state, 3, 13, 27, 71, 101–2, 138, 156
Mezzogiorno, investment in, 52–3

micro-economics: theory, 103, 140, 168; policies, 137, 196–8
migrant labour, 167, 172–4, 207 *note* 3; emigrant, 87–8, 95; immigrant, 72, 88–9, 95, 98
minimum wages, 21, 97, 191
Ministry of Finance (France), 10, 19, 22
monetarism, 4, 101, 129, 158, 182
monetary policy, 87–8, 99, 128, 141, 182
Monnet, Jean, 13–15
monopoly: trend, 3, 28, 139–42, 148, 168–72; policies against, 78–9, 93, 97, 139–50 *passim*; problems, 3, 140–1, 156, 169–72; *see also* meso-economic sector, nationalization
multinational companies, 135–6, 158, 168; trend to, 139–42, 148, 168–72; problems, 135–6, 140–1, 153, 169–72; *see also* meso-economic sector, nationalization

National Economic Development Council *see* NEDC
National Enterprise Board *see* NEB
National Hydrocarbons Corporation (ENI), 52, 136
National Plan (UK), 126–9, 137, 139
nationalization, 3, 14, 31–2, 36–9, 45, 106, 108, 133, 134–6, 147, 149; *see also* public enterprise
nationalized industries, 14, 39, 52–3, 134, 149
NEB (National Enterprise Board), 134, 138, 142, 146–52 *passim*

NEDC (National Economic Development Council), 50, 123–6, 127, 147

negotiation, social (between state, management and unions), 11, 15–16, 18, 24, 40, 43, 99, 113–14, 123–4, 147, 185, 192–6, 199–200

Oil: prices and OPEC, 1, 2, 5, 12, 85, 122, 132, 142–3, 153, 175; sector, 135–6, 154

Orientierungsrahm (SPD Long-Term Programme) 110–17

Parliament, 58, 186, 195, 200–1; parliamentary sovereignty, 155–6

Pieraccini Plan (Italy, 1966–70), 50–3

Planning Agreements: Britain, 134, 138–9, 142, 146–52, 200; French and Belgian prototypes, 211 *note* 3; Italy (*contrattazione programmatica*), 51–3

'Planning for Progress' (Balogh), 126–7, 210 *note* 4

political crisis/demands, 158–61, 180–4; France, 12–13, 22–5, 29, 109, 159–60; Germany, 109–10, 117; Italy, 71–4, 80–1, 159–60; *see also* industrial democracy, social democracy

price policies, 21–3, 197–8; controls, 121, 131, 143–5

prices, 86, 157, 177, 182, 208 *note* 5; commodity, 132, 143, 154, 166; oil, 1, 2, 5, 12, 85, 122, 132, 142–3, 153; meso-economic sector's price-making power, 70, 140–2, 169–72, 174–5

profits, 36, 44, 56, 86, 88, 90, 109, 143–4, 154, 185; and meso-economic sector, 70–1, 73, 140–2, 169–72, 174, 180

Progetto Ottanta (Project for the Eighties, Italy), 54

Progetto Quadro (Programme Structure/Project Framework, Italy), 54, 63–4

Programme Contracts system, 137–8

public enterprise, 3–4, 32, 51–3, 134–6, 138, 142, 147–50, 154, 158; *see also* nationalization

public expenditure, 1–2, 11, 19, 27–8, 149, 176–9; planning, 35, 70–1, 111, 176, 184–95 *passim*, 198–201; restraint, 4–6, 36, 123, 143–5, 154, 157–9; *see also* social expenditure, state aids and incentives, 'stop-go' policies

public ownership *see* nationalization

Rationalization, 90, 207 *note* 2

recession, 36, 52, 87, 90, 97, 100, 109, 117, 131, 167, 175, 180, 192; *see also* capitalist crisis

reflation, 5, 182, 192

regions: problems, 49, 51–3, 192; policies, 12, 26, 64–5, 76, 78, 100, 149, 191–2, *contrattazione programmatica*, 51–3

resource allocation and distribution, 11, 14, 16, 19, 29, 43–4, 73, 111, 134, 137, 145, 156, 176, 184, 187, 191–2; *see also* investment, Planning Agreements, public enterprise, public expenditure, redistribution *under* incomes, social

resource allocation and distribution—*cont.*
accounting, social expenditure, social indicators
revaluation of Deutschmark *see under* Deutschmark

Saving, 18, 97, 165, 188; propensity to save, 91, 207 *note* 3
Second French Plan, 17–20
second Italian five-year plan (1973–7, not adopted), 54–5
self-management, 29–33, 37–44, 58, 72–81 *passim*; *see also* decentralization of planning
social accounting, 58–65, *tables* 65–8, 192–202 *passim*; see also social indicators
social costs and benefits *see* redistribution *under* incomes, social accounting, social expenditure, social indicators
Social Democratic Party (Germany) *see* SPD
social democracy, 29–30, 38–40, 78–81, 158–61, 182–5; *see also* democracy and planning; industrial democracy; negotiation, social
social expenditure, 5–6, 19–23, 27–8, 71, 149, 176–9, 184–94, 198–202; *see also* social accounting, social indicators, social security transfers *under* social security
social indicators, 30, 54, 56–65, *tables* 65–8, 78, 187, 194; *see also* social accounting
social market philosophy, 92–3, 97–8, 100, 107–10, 114–16
social security, 14, 36, 72, 92,

184; social security transfers, 20–1, 76, 177–9, 185, 188
Socialist Party (France), 38–9
Socialist Party (Italy), 50
socialist planning, 4–6, 185–202; Britain, 133–5, 137–9, 148–50, 156–8; France, 29–33, 37–46; Germany, 110–17; Italy, 55–68, 74–81
socialization of means of production *see* nationalization
SPD (German Social Democratic Party), 98, 104, 106, 108; Godesberg Programme (1959), 108–10; *Orientierungsrahm* (Long-Term Programme), 110–14, 117; Mannhein Programme (1975), 114–15; relationship with trade unions, 109–10, 115–16
Stability Act (1967), 98–100
Stabilization Plan (France), 20
state aids and incentives: for investment, 14–15, 18, 27, 51, 86, 89, 99, 104, 113, 145, 177, 192, 195; social security transfers, 20–1, 76, 177–9, 185, 188
state capitalism, 3, 60–1, 72, 102; *see also* nationalization, public enterprise
State Holding Companies, 137–8, 147
state intervention, 1–6 *passim*, 187; in Britain, 133–4, 137, 158; in France, 1, 9–10, 14–15, 34–7, 41; in Germany, 97, 99–100, 104–5, 108; in Italy, 51–3, 70–1; *see also* competition policies, demand management, fiscal policy, incomes policies, monetary policy,

State intervention—*cont.*
nationalization, Planning Agreements, public enterprise, public expenditure, resource allocation and distribution, state aids and incentives
state ownership *see* nationalization, public enterprise
sterling devaluation, 121, 125–6, 128–9, 137, 141, 210 *note* 4
'stop-go' policies, 123, 125, 129, 167–8, 175; *see also* incomes policies
structural unemployment *see under* unemployment

Taxation, 1, 18, 21, 99, 130, 135, 143–4, 154, 179, 185, 188–9, 191; reducing personal taxation, 158, 179; subsidies/relief, 3–4, 27, 86, 89, 104, 143, 145, 154, 177, 191
trade: balance of, 13, 20, 88, 93–7, 122–3, 126, 131–2, 153; invisible, 94; visible, 88, 93–5, *table* 94, *table* 95, 140–1, 153; *see also* balance of payments, exports, imports
trade unions: and incomes policies, 21–2, 70–2, 98, 144–6, 151; and planning role, 16, 31–2, 40, 58, 63, 78, 80, 109–11, 113–14, 115–16, 130, 150–2, 153, 180, 185–6, 193; and Planning Agreements, 51, 138–9, 142, 146, 150; *see also* negotiation, social
transfer pricing, 142, 170, 198
transport, 19, 39, *chart* 68, 89, 176, 178, 189
Treasury, 122, 124–5, 127–9, 143
TUC, 144, 146, 152–3, 155

Under-consumption, 86, 89, 91, 158
undervaluation of Deutschmark *see under* Deutschmark
unemployment, 1, 24, 26, 71–2, 85–8 *passim*, 101, 117, 125–30 *passim*, 153, 167; structural, 3, 36, 90, 96, 111, 116, 157, 165, 173, 182, 184–5, 190; *see also* employment
United States, 12, 36, 89, 96, 108, 125, 142, 148, 166
urbanization, 24, 76, 191; urban planning, 19, 43, 76, 78, 191
use values, 42, 44

'Value planning', 20–2
'Vanoni Plan' (Italy), 49
visible trade, 88, 93–5, *table* 94, *table* 95, 140–1, 153

Wages *see* incomes
wages policies / restraint *see* incomes policies
wealth distribution, 40, 107, 180; *see also* incomes
welfare state, 72–4, 154, 166, 176–9, 189; *see also* public expenditure, social expenditure, social security
Wilson, Sir Harold, 121, 126, 130, 139, 143, 147, 152; *The Four Year Plan, quoted* 127
Wirtschaftwunder, 86–92 *passim*
workers' control, 40, 80, 107–8, 115, 150, 156–7, 198; *see also* decentralization of planning; democracy and planning; industrial democracy; negotiation, social; political crisis/demands; self-management; social democracy